The Astrologer's Dog

Ivarna and me, by Florence

days in the life of an astrologer, Ivarna, and her dog, Florence

The Astrologer's Dog
Ivarna and me, by Florence

Ivarna Kalinova

First published in Great Britain 2016 by
Purple Inkwell Books
isbn 978-0-9567454-2-2

Contents

introduction

Florence is a very special Chow-Chow. Born in the Welsh countryside and brought up by the sea in the North of England, this amazing dog has been a part of Ivarna's the life for the past 9 years. Having had a few ups and downs, Florence has presented Ivarna with some difficult times, yet has continued to fill the astrologer's day with endless joy.

I have been fortunate to have shared Ivarna's life for many years and no matter how dark the day Florence can bring a sparkle to Ivarna's tired eyes with just a nose to her knee and a look that says, "time we went walkies."

Ivarna was going to write this book, but I suggested Florence do it, as she knows how it really feels, and Ivarna has plenty to keep her busy as it is. So this is how it was through the dark eyes of Florence.

This is not a work of fiction, it is the real life story of Ivarna, the astrologer, and her dog, Florence, with a little astrology of dogs thrown in. There are fearful days when we thought her life was almost over, visits to various vet's in search of hope, with tears of sorrow, and joy, and surprise, and mindful walks on windswept beaches. I know this book has given Ivarna and myself much inspiration and a new way of looking at life with a dog. I hope you find it an enjoyable read, and perhaps offer strength to those going through tough times with their own pet.

Alex

puppy days

I was born with a destiny. An astrologer's dog is unlike any other dog. I remember the first time out of the big house gate. It was early winter As I squatted to pee there was a tinge of frosting on the grass, the red brick path of the garden felt cold under my warm puppy paws. It was early winter. My soft short puppy lead was dropped over my head, the squeaking creak of the little rusted iron gate and we were through it onto a wide pavement. It was the first time out of the garden. Unlike most dogs I didn't sniff the slabs from curiosity, to see who'd walked there. I was too stunned. The cacophony of noise, of people, of cars, the sights, the sounds. The post mans red barrow being wheeled up the pavement towards me. The big van being unloaded next door, with its thumping and banging and laughing men in overalls. The voices of children. Stark daylight, Lampposts. Bus stops. The strange dank smell of salt air and screeching of the gulls. This was nothing like the quiet country place where I was born. I turned struggling to run back into the sanctuary of the garden and house. My owners face close to me, voice coaxing, hand caressing head "Florence, come, this way. We'll only walk as far as next doors gate!" People bending down at me, all eyes and faces. Shoes, wooly socks and winter boots. The world stopping for me, quieting for me. The collective "Aaahh look at the puppy, its like a Teddy bear". Then the barrage of noise again, the never ending discordant orchestra of the life and breath of a city street, The phrazes "First time out the house" seeming to be echoed by owner and others alike. The world here was a kaleidoscope of sound, colour, moving things, people, very different to the one I was used to.

I was still little enough then to be picked up and kissed on the forehead when we were back in our own garden. I was exhausted. The fascinating. half frightening sounds and sights of a myriad moving things. The smells and sights and colours of the place drifting in the air. I lapped at my breakfast. Then I lay straight down where I was and went to sleep for hours. Dreamed jumbled up things" Its going to take forever to get you to go round the block" she said. She was wrong, within two more days I was confident enough to pass the house next door and several others, and leave our rusted black gate far behind. Within two weeks I was happily tugging my owner round the far corner, full of life and curiosity. Exploring the strangeness of this

3

patchwork place. The world opened up and swallowed me in wonder, I had no time to fret for all the things I'd left behind.

Things come into my mind dimly, like a muted light in a dark room, a kind of instinctive knowing. Some things are old beyond memory. A stirring within me, an intuitive understanding. I know what's said to me, not word for word, but impression, meanings, thoughts seep from the fog. I understand conversations but not the detail of them, words flow past me like water. I feel the substructure of what's being said. I pick out the odd word that has special meanings to me, like Walk, Bowl, Lead, Garden. I know the difference between the word 'yard' and the word 'garden'. I absorb everything around me, like water through wool. An urge to growl or a bark grows unbidden within my rib cage, from some alien unsettling sound, usually a human voice. I recognise the regular routine sounds, they fade into my background, but old as I am voices still disturb me. I understand the words "Shut up, and shush Florence" but cannot master the command instantly for my instincts compel a bark but my conscious mind wants to obey a command, I struggle between willfulness and obedience but I know what it all means. I know what many words mean. This is what its like to be a dog.

A week or two after I came to live with Ivarna, we were walking back from the park at the end of our street. It was my habit when the pavement was empty to canter ahead on my extending walk lead, it was down hill all the way, and so we gained momentum. If people appeared in the path my lead was quickly shortened in however and by the time we reached them, or they came past us, I was pulled to the side and had to walk close in to Ivarna's legs. If I saw an open garden gate in passing, I would try and go in. "No, Florence, has to be your own house, anybody's house gate won't do" She'd say. I quite liked the glimpses of other gardens, other windows. I think Ivarna did too. That particular day. I was a just little ahead crossing the road at the corner when I stumbled at the curb, ." Oops Florence!" My lead and head were quickly jerked up in the nick of time, prevented me hitting my chin, and righting my body". We stopped instantly, my ankles were rubbed, my big mitts of front paws looked at, my chin lifted. Football face rubbed. We carried on "What caused that I wonder?" She said to me, she always talked to me. The pavements were looked at to see if there was wonky slab, or any stumbling block, a little

4

puppy could trip on. There wasn't one. One was smooth and grey, the other like current cake. One was beginning to crack, there was nothing at all I could have tripped on. But soon after I stumbled again, this time in the house. " She's careless with her feet" Alex said, another new word. My days were full and joyful while Ivarna worked long hours often way into the night, she worked from our own home so she had plenty of time for me. It's a fine thing to be an astrologer's dog.

My hair is thick and coarse, its mostly a red gold, though some of its sandy fair and cream and it's sweeping-brush long, but longer and stiffer round my hackles and lion mane head. My tail curls up on my back like a tea pot handle and has a long plume of cream colour. My belly has some cream too, And my face is like a lion. When I was young I had eyes of dark amber but just this year they have darkened into wise old brown eyes, and like all of my race I have a purple tongue. I am a sturdy dog, a solid dog. I have nice fat feet like fur slippers and my fetlocks can be combed out to resemble those of a cart horse. I am a Chow-Chow, and also a Florence. Anyone who has had to learn a foreign language knows it's daunting and confusing at first. I learned quickly. I learned I am a " Chow Chow" and I learned I'm a "Florence". I am also a "Good dog," a" Good lass", and a sometimes "what breed is it?" and a "ahh, I've never seen one of them before!" and "by'e that's a nice dog, you've got there, what's her name?" "Florence". I'm a "Florence." When I reached the ankle biting stage of puppy hood, I learned some other new words, but I have I cannot repeat them here. An astrologers dog is a wise old dog who knows a lot, like the good Astrologer herself I know more than I can ever say

Puppy days are happy days. in my new life I see things I never have before. In the park there is a lake with flocks of swans, in the winter the water is half covered with Ice and the park is empty and the are crowds of swans on the path at the edges of the lake and in the pink fading late afternoon early evening light and it really is like a scene from a ballet. Ivarna ties me to a tree or a seat sometimes, and the bread bag comes out and as she walks along the edge of the water they all follow her like a drove of white sheep, and the gulls white and silver winged fly down from above, cart wheeling, swooping and screaming overhead They have learned to catch crumbs in mid air. I watch the swans on the path looming closer, beaks reaching down to

5

her bag black waddling feed like rubber legs, being thrown a crust as she backs away, or sometimes gingerly handed one. There is a crowded street of shops, that smells of a thousand things, cloth and meat pasties and people, and flooded with the sound of voices, and clangs and shouts, and street music, where I see more shoes walking up and down and people in them than I have ever seen in my life before. My eyes are wide with wonder I sit and watch them. I am introduced to passing children, and dogs, and tables. I get used to everything. One day we watch the ferry boat coming in an out, we are sitting on the jetty, with he sound of the industrial hammers and the ships hooters and smells of fish and seaweed, wafting in the fresh salt air and another day we are up on the platform watching the metro train. " Now you know what everything is" She says. And I do.

Memorys fade and merge and all are one eventually. My mother Grace was beautifull. I have only a dim memory of her and the picture in Ivarna's mind to draw from. Over the years I am not sure what is real., what was dreamed. In the photograph she looks like me. But in my memory her hair was redder than mine, like a ruby red fire. Burning bright. She was young my mother, young and carefree. Happy and warm to snuggle into, she had all a dog could ever want, even puppies. But she rejected me. She didn't want me. You could say I was born an orphan. Ivarna says all of us are alone, all of us are islands when it comes down to it. We learn to survive. But a puppy needs love and warmth more than most. That's when my human mother Jenny took over, she bottle fed me. She was beautifull too. Jenny and Ivarna merge into one in my mind. They were both yellow haired, fair and thin with long tapering fingers and hands. It hands I remember from my puppy days. Hands coming towards me. The carpet was the same. That Chinese carpet with the turquoise and cream pattern, soft and warm on my paws, smelling of wool, it was in both houses, like the yellow hair and the hands the memorys merge, strangely, it is here and there and yet they are not the same place. There is a black dog too, a big looming dark face thrust into mine like a memory or it may be a ghost I see in Ivarna's mind. It is called George or Ziggy.

Things permeate into me like sunlight on my skin What to do, what not to do? I am not an obedient dog, there is nothing of the people-pleaser or hand-licker in me. I have never welcomed a stranger, or relative or anyone into Ivarna's house, my house. But I've never bitten one either. I am calm and intelligent. I have heard these word applied to me. I'm a slow dog., an observant dog, its deep in my nature, my breed and ancestry. I watch, I think, I act. A girl with soft, sniffable, suede boots, who smells of flowers, and talks to Ivarna at our gate says 'I used to live next door to two big chows, they would lie on the step in the summer, someone would knock on the door , about five minutes later they would get up and bark' "Yes, that about sums a chow up", Ivarna says. I don't bark at her, an arm as slender as a swans neck and softly coated in grey wool snakes over gate, and my ears are tickled delightfully. "How old is she?" How old am I? "Nearly a year" Ivarna says. Time is a mystery to me, but to an astrologer it is an all important measurement. Dogs have horoscopes too, as does everything on earth, and to draw any horoscope you need the time and date and place of birth to make it unique. Most people think its only zodiac signs, but real astrology is far more complex. Dogs charts cannot be read in the same way as human charts, but they can be read. Being an astrologer's dog mine was consulted often in my puppy days. But then it seemed to get left in the back of the draw.

There is a café in the park, It resembles a Nordic timber cabin, looking onto the lake. Occasionally in the Winter when its quiet we sit at table outside, and Ivarna drinks a coffee. She Lies me down, wraps my lead twice round my neck tucks it over my back and round the table leg. "Stay there Florence" and to the people sitting at the table opposite she will say. " Can you watch my dog doesn't walk away with the table please." My curiosity wants to follow her inside to the counter. I'm fooled into thinking I am anchored so I stay put.

A park gardener has a conversation with me that begins "Hello doggy'" I have sat down on the damp grass fascinated because, he is doing the exactly the same mysterious thing Ivarna does at home. Poking little orange petalled plants into the ground. It is beyond my comprehension. Its an intelligent dog that sits and watches the world Ivarna thinks, so I don't disillusion her with a questioning look. There are things abounding in the human world that are not easily explained, they are as mysterious to me as the sky at night. I see them all on my way round. These human mystery, my turgid brain hardly makes sense of them, it is just how things are, accepted and noted. I store them in the cupboard of memory without knowing what they are, the same as I pack away other things, the sting of a nettle, the house where a bigger dog lives. I know what to avoid and what doesn't matter. Ivarna smiles at the gardener and tries to tug me on, but when ever I sit down, I'm sat or "parked herself and wouldn't budge" as she will later tell Alex. Ivarna cannot move me on, the old yank on the collar is ineffective, the words doled out like sweets don't work either. All the 'come-on's and 'good dog's. The harder tugs, still she cannot budge me, I am much too heavy. A bulldozer couldn't move me on. We wait till I'm ready, until my attention at this new curiosity wanders and my interest wanes, and I'm up and off again . All our walks are pleasant and interesting like this.

I am neither stubborn, nor difficult she says but I don't do as I'm told. The great dark face lingers in my mind, known but unknown. Suddenly I know. She was my predecessor this great jet dark beast. And I realize other things dimly. Ivarna thinks I might be beyond her strength, that I might be her last big or bulky dog, her last Chow, she has a weak back and a whole dog's life older now than when she lead trained this other dog I am not really that big, but I'm solid and sturdy and wide. Its hard to lead train a powerfull dog if your not physically strong yourself. I feel all her uncertainties drift in the air between us but there are no regrets, and I am learning to be softer, I no longer snatch at treats and toys, I take them more carefully from her hands. I soft nose her, with a nudge when I want her attention, or pat her with my big mitted paws. I don't nip anymore. I don't barge through her so much, I know to wait. When I take her for a walk on the lead, she is reluctant to hurry, she drags herself along, she is always lagging behind me like a dead weight , a sack of potatoes on my collar. I have to pull and haul her along you'd think shed be keen and excited like me to get out wouldn't you, a way from the other great weight, the work. The work is a less physical weight but it is endless. Sometimes she just stands there, yes, parks herself. While I haul away, looking back at her over my hackles, trying to see what the hold up is, and saying silently come on Ivarna, move yourself !. I have no option but to wait until she un-parks herself then off we go.

She spent a long time training me to walk at her side, she has never succeeded. I am a chow I walk in front. She says it is sufficient not to pull. One day she was shopping in Newcastle's Grainger market, I was at home but mentally I followed her round. She used to go to the butchers and go fumbling through his bone bags, carefully selecting a bag of little meaty bones that were just the right size for my mouth, she know exactly what I like. That day a guide dog pup was being trained in the market. Much fussed over by the butcher. " Nice dogs labs, I've got an Alsatian pup myself. " he said to Ivarna " I've got a chow, but I'm having a job getting her not pull on the lead. I don't think I could manage an Alsatian, it would have me over!". "He's quite strong big for his age, but they are very obedient you know." "How do you train him not to pull? "Easy, when we are in the house, I keep his collar and lead on, and I tie it to my leg, where I go the dog goes. When I turn the corner the dog turns the corner, when I sit I make the dog sit. It keep him at my side and he learns all the time. When I let him off the lead on our outdoor walk he hardly strays from my side.

But already I am too strong, you'd need legs like tree trunks, or like the butcher's, to do that method. The treat and reward method doest work either. I am not that interested in treats Ivarna thinks I works but only works on hungry dogs', I am a fat fully fed on good stuff puppy. I get a harness. It is supposed to stop pulling, but Ivarna find it harder, it hurts her back more. I get a head collar, rather like a horses, except there is no " bit" in the mouth. I find paw to nose, takes the muzzle part it off. So I paw to nose all the way up the garden path, out of the gate, and up the street and round the corner, Ivarna bends and bobs up and down all the way like an animated nodding doll, putting it back over my snout. every few seconds. But she likes it, because all the paw over nose and sniffling round drain pipes trying to push my muzzle strap off slows me down. " We'll persevere Florence, we will try again tomorrow". She tightens it up so I cannot paw it off. I have to snidge it off against next doors gate post, and then against the wall, and against the curb and then the lamppost. She preservers for several weeks, but we never get as far as the park in it. We are supposed to walk on quickly to distract the dog, so it forgets it has it on, but I wont walk quickly. I never forget I've got it on. I wont budge, and just as Ivarna has to make a great physical effort to hold me back when I pull her along the road, so she has to make an equally vast physical effort to get me move forward when I want to stand still.

9

Ivarna is wearing a long narrow dark drab skirt, its not my favourite its too smooth against my nose, and there is no whiff of scented washing powder emanating from it, but I find I can use that and her knee joint like the gate post to snidge the head collar off. Is very handy because it's a movable post. When I'm not near a gate post or a fence post or curb or the hundred other things I find to rub my nose against, I turn into Ivarna's knee bone instead. It saves me lifting my paw. Sometimes we do a pirouette on the pavement. Her knee trying to keep out of the way of my snout, and my nose following the knee to snitch my muzzle off. In the weeks that follow, I paw it off, snidge it off, wipe it off, walk backwards out of it altogether. Then I do the unthinkable, I suddenly I shoot across the pavement, to a passing man, and with my nose I snidge the offending head collar it off against his trousers. Ivarna doesn't know where to put herself. . We make it safely back round the corner . We are very close to being home, when I see another pair of trousers and head off to repeat myself. Ivarna with a firm hand gets hold of my scruff and arrests my progress.. Next day I'm back on my old ancestral leather it belonged to Ziggy before me, so its nicely worn into shape, its roll shaped not flat, its smooth on my neck but strong and chunky, collar and attaches to my red lead " She's just at the difficult Stage " Ivarna says.

training sessions

One morning the clattering sound of the letter box flapping and the thump of the mail on the floor interrupts my slumber I go to grab a letter while Ivarna scoops up an armful of mail and removes the letter from my mouth and we go back down the hall. The usual client letters and catalogues , flyers from the curry house, bills, cards, and a small cream envelope. She sits down beside me on the stairs with it. While I look at it curiously. Knowing in the way dogs know without being told that there is something different. Ivarna smiles at me, opens it theatrically with a flourish in front of my face and puts the letter immediately to my nose. I soak up the smell and something stirs, I wrestle with my elusive memories. I look at her. I try to get a mouth hold on the swirling fleeting glimpses. I see Ginger my playfull sister, and suddenly just for a second I'm back in the knot of my first family, the feeling of fur on my face, the closeness of other dogs, the knowledge that I'm not alone, safe, secure, surrounded in the warmth of my little dog family, the other Ivarna beside me, the other dark Ziggy but in a blink of the eye its gone again. What kind of magic is this, that half transports me through time and back. I sniff again but nothing more transpires. The door is shut. The past is a place you cannot go, except by chance.

My mind is heaped over with impressions, disconnected remnants and feelings, that resonate with deeper unknown things , they are in no particular order. but within me, like a poignant melody that touches and evokes something beyond itself. Some feeling or thought was retrieved by the letter, something known, but is gone now like a fish slipping back into the merky pool again.

"It's from Jenny" Ivarna says, " I wish I was telepathic like you, Florence, then I could tell you about Jenny and your family," she continues anyway, "Jenny hasn't heard from Muffin's owner, so we don't know how your brother is getting on. He has moved away like the black sheep of the family and we know nothing of how his fortunes are now, if he's well, if he's happy."

I think in meanings, I cannot think in words or in pictures. I just know things holistically, part of me is in tune with the collective, the earth,

11

and the universe, Ivarna can think this way too, think in meanings, perception come to her, a significant knowing that is infinitely different from guessing or imagining, hazy dream like impressions from the collective darkness. She includes these in some of her astrology readings ,but only when she is sure. Infallibly it astounds her clients. It works in her own life too this strange knowing but her human logic blocks it out in every day life. The human mind always seeks to make order from disorder.. This book is translated into words for me, from dog think to human language and abridged so that humans can comprehend it. If I appear too human in this book it is because words are not adequate to mimic my dog thoughts and because I know no names of items I think, I feel, I recall but I do not reason .

"You have forgotten to let Florence see you leave the house." Alex calls to Ivarna, as she picks up her dark brown bag, strap over shoulder, the bag that smells of polish and goatskin and paper all the things inside of it. The light blue jacket is flung on and the great door opens, the outside world floods in light daylight.

"If she doesn't see you go out of the front door, she will wander round the rooms all day looking for you. But of you make sure she sees you go, she will settle down quite happy by the stairs untill you come back" Alex adds. Ivarna is bemused by this news, but she knows instantly it's right. She looks for me, I turn and walk, my chops are slopping water after drinking from my steel water bowl. She plants a kiss on her first two fingers and puts it to my cheek. " Bye Bye, Florence, be a good girl!"

Slowly in stages Ivarna learns how I think and we communicate better. I am like the small child who thinks if he cannot see his mother, his mother cannot see him. Abstract concepts are partly meaningless to me. Nor does reason come automatically.. Every ragged detail of my life, the smells and sounds and textures, the things I have seen, fears and desires and urges, every responses from a million new experiences are stored unsorted in a messy tangle in my mind. Things permeate back up to the surface as if drawn there, compelled by the daylight to become known again. If a thing frightens me one time, its imprint frightens me the next. What I do once, I will do again. To me nothing is ever separated. I am a different dog from Ziggy and from Flash, the grey hound she used to mind for his owners. The structures of our mind and thinking are all different

Ivarna goes out often. She calls it doing shopping, its like hunting or foraging. Comes back with shapeless cotton bag of things. It sags on the floor and I nose while she takes off her jacket. Vegetables, that hold no interest for me. The soily smell of potatoes and leafy green cabbage. Little toys for me and Alex to amuse ourselves, mince meat, a wedge of cheese. Something red and wooly. There is always something worthwhile in the bag. Once it was a tennis ball for me. Another time it was a bouncing toy. This time my anticipation is not rewarded a book slides out in her hand "Went to the library got a dog training book" She says brightly.

"We should have trained earlier, when she was tiny, how did you lead train Ziggy?" Alex says, as if to jog an answer out of the memory pot. He mistakenly thinks what works on one dog works on all. " Ziggy was a different dog. Right from the beginning she was a snuffler, nose to the ground sniffer dawdling down the path. So I never discouraged that. There was no " walk on". I let her collar hand slack. Stood still waited while she sniffed, we went along together because every few steps shed be sniffling at something. So I thought that's good, encourage that, no pulling your arm out of its socket. When she did walk too far ahead 'Id just yank the lead a little, and shed slow or stop and wait for me. She always walked in front of course chows always do, but Florence surges ahead like a big tank, pulling me along behind, you'd think she was going for first in a cart and trotters race.!"

We practice other training methods in the back yard. Its great fun! Alex reads from a book, that instructs the owner to put the lead on it, walk off briskly, and as soon as the dog gets ahead abruptly turn in the opposite direction. Walking quickly at an angle, or back the way you came. The dog will follow, it says. Each time it surges ahead you repeat this stark sudden change of direction. Then stand still and the dog will wait to see which way your going and will follow. " It probably works on spaniels, and terriers,, little dogs " She says doubtfully.

Ivarna finds I'm quicker than her, I have four fast legs, she has two, she doesn't get the chance to 'walk off briskly ahead of me' because I always walk off first and I'm always in front and if she could find the strength to keep me still long enough, or yank me back, she wouldn't be needing the book she says.

She tries the fast change of directions manouver she manages to keep her balance skidding on the cobbles, and calling to me, despite her arm and shoulder being jolted backwards by the lead as she turns and I carry on straight ahead regardless. Its a good game. I get the hang of it and we do a few clockwise ever decreasing circles because as soon as Ivarna changes direction I'm round and in front again, so she turns again and I'm instantly in front again, I go quicker and quicker, I am so enjoying this game.. It a bit like playing lampposts. It filters into my thoughts that it is like lampposts without the lamp. So I decide to pull Ivarna round and lead her in a few quick anticlockwise circles. Like we do when we wind the lead round the lamppost and I have to "Come round Florence" to unwind it. Its complicated, takes an intelligent chow like me to know I have to come back round the lamp post but I sometimes even I get it wrong, so Ivarna has to go round the lamppost the opposite way to unwind it. If I try to help and go round the same time as she is going round to unwind, we end up with the lead wrapped three times round the lamp post. This yard game is a bit like that. I like games " Oh dear, she's never going to learn, and her such an intelligent dog" Ivarna says..

Then there is a glimmer in the dark attic of Ivarna's head. " Ah! I know what it is!" she gushes at me. The dawn of realization in a human mind is a wonderfull thing for a dog to watch. It shows on the face. I kept looking at her face after that, incase I might one day see it again. Some dogs never see it in the whole of their existence, and their lives turn into regimented robotic dogs. Do this, do that do it a thousand times until you can do nothing else but obey. " I need a long bit of thin rope, like a clothes line. I need to be able to attach it to her collar" She says to Alex. She virtually jumps up and down with anticipation. I stood next to Ivarna's chair. Like a toddler at a mothers knee, watching my first extended lead being made, it consisted of three of the longest dog leads she could find fastened clipped on to each other. " It just right" She said. I wagged in encouragement and anticipation at the prospective walk. " What it is," she said to Alex

" She thinks she's doing what I want. I pull her, so she pulls me!. She's a Libra you know. Libras dogs can be stubborn occasionally but they are never rebellious. They are protective, playful appreciate affection, and they learn by copying. If you have a favourite old dog who behaves just the way you want and are used to, and you want a puppy so as to have something when he's gone, a Libra is a good choice of pup. It will learn more from copying your old dog, than you could ever teach it".

The long lead worked for both of us. The walks were less of a game of tug. In empty back lanes and stretches of beach and grass, I made my own pace. Ivarna kept hers. The further ahead I was, the less effort she had to put into yanking me to a slow down. It became just a twitch of her wrist, not a two handed lean back ward immense effort job " Must be the dynamics of the thing" She said to Alex. I was always an impatient dog, I liked my new lead that let me go ahead. Id stop now and again and look behind to make sure she was still following. Id never done that before, but it seemed necessary now, to stop and look I'd see her lace up boots and her short quick little clipped steps, her ankle grazer skirts, she no longer broke into a long stride that hurt her back, or be jolted along the avenues trying to keep me close. Then I'd raise my face and see her face smiling at me. it warmed me. This lead was the first of many. It would be interchanged with my ordinary walking lead, for the high street, or busy pavement times. Some days we'd walk further than others, but always whether it was a long walk or short one, the walk was my favourite part of my day.

In the park we go from seat to seat, Ivarna trailing behind like a weedy old woman and wincing when I jolt the lead in my keenness to get ahead. I squint up at her as only a chow can. I want to understand. I am like a foreigner thrown into a strange world where I cannot speak the language. I am like someone whose lost his memory and has to start again. She talks to me, as if I am human. Occasionally I whine back. She knows a whine is a want. A want to communicate." Talking to a dog keeps them calm and focus their attention on you", she says." I've got a bad back today Florence, so we are going to have to sit down a lot" we pick our way though the park, seat to seat. I grasp this quickly and soon wherever we go I know to find Ivarna a seat, sometimes it's a rock, a great stone, a rubbish bin, a bike stand, a sewage pipe. "What a good dog you are Florence."

On a frozen day we both slip on the ice in the park path and I don't pull onward. I stop I wait until she gets up. Finds her feet, she hangs on to a tree and I proceed with caution. I'm a good dog, good dog Florence. Suddenly I'm down again, feet flaying, skidding. I'm up, we decide to leave the icy path pick our way crunching over the grass and under the trees. No words exchange, we just cooperate. I retain this in my memory and one summers day as we leave the house she say" now be good Florence my back is very bad today, and I get it, walk the perfect walk. I wait for her I don't pull. I keep looking at her, I'm not distracted when we pass other dogs, I totally ignore them, I can feel her utter puzzlement. " It's as if she understands, but other days its like she regresses to a puppy having a game of tug, I yank her back she yanks me forwards, the tail wags at every yank, and she thinks it's a great game!" She looks for explanations and non is forthcoming." She going to be such a good dog isn't she. She's just taken a bit longer to learn" she says to Alex..

On the first memorable day that we go beyond the park, it is a wonderfull in indescribable desert. Where the ground is soft and yellow for walking and the water draws you toward it and the air is pure salt and the sound of the river and ships drift over. Something old and primitive in me knows this place. It is the desert. "It's the beach Florence. We can only come here in winter because in summer its off limits to dogs, but winter is better because its not full of people," I find her an upturned tree trunk to sit on, and my lead is changed from, the walking lead, is unhooked, and a thin black cord that light and free, stretches forever is put on my collar. I run down to the waters edge to play. There are little coloured stones, I sniff the salt and seaweed small of them, poke them with my paw, foamy white water like the frill of a lace curtains edge washes over my feet and trickles suddenly down between my toes. I wag my tail in delight. I sit beside Ivarna, then I am down to the into water again, we walk along the tide line in the sea, out of the sea waves wash me into the shore, then its "Come on Florence we'll have to go back and get some work done. There is two one year forecasts to do, and someone wants me to see if I can get anything about her Career prospects." My lead is

16

changed back to the walk lead, the other one is coiled up wet and dripping and stuffed into a plastic bag, and back we go. An astrologers life is a busy one. We reach the house, the garden gate, I soon know my own house.

For a dog, the garden gate is the doorway into the world. In astrology the ascendant is the threshold of life. It is the doorway to the whole chart. But to know what degree and constellation is on your ascendant, you have to know the precise hour and minute of your birth, as well as the date and place. Once you know that, you can open the gate of your chart and look into the future, the past, the different avenues of life that surround you.

A "House" in an astrological chart is not a house you live in with roofs to keep out the rain and windows and stoves and bowls full of fresh water and tables to sleep under. An astrological house isn't warm, its vast and cold as the universe, its a portion or division of the sky. There are twelve houses, a whole streets worth in an astrological chart. Century's ago most astrologers decided the sixth celestial house was the house of pets, while some astrologers thought the fifth house befitted a pet better. There is still disagreement to this day between astrological sources. All I can tell you is what Ivarna found, that my picture is portrayed most excellently by her fifth house.

Astrologically Planet Mercury in my chart, the messenger planet, which rules the voice, the mind, communication, the ears, nervous system conjuncts with Ivarna's Neptune in her chart. Neptune is the psychic planet. Astrologically it means a kind of knowing, we pick up undercurrents unspoken things, signs from each other. If Ivarna's was a dog we would have a vague telepathy, but as human her mind is hindered by human-ness so she has to settle for a kind of knowing. Humans know both everything and nothing. I wouldn't care to be a human..

My chart is drawn up and frequently consulted. This is not meant to be an astrology book, but astrology ran through our life every day like the stitches that hold a garment together, and being an astrologers dog, these things got discussed. A dogs birth date is sometimes known but its time is often not. So like a human who doesn't know his hour of birth there are many compromises in a dogs chart. I am a Libra but I love the water, isn't that strange, so after that first discovery of wonderful water can be we go to Little Haven beach often. We watch the tides wash in and out and always the scene changes, one autumn there is a load of tree logs and branches washed up and they line the beach all winter.

ghosts of the past

I get a variety of succulent meaty food for my meals. When I was puppy, my first home raised me up on rice and chicken. At Ivarna's home that was my staple diet for a long time. I got through three scrawny green market chickens and a big bag of rice, a packet of sausages and two slices of fried bread, and a bone a week . The sound of the rice bubbling on the hob and the whir of the turntable in the microwave going round wafting chicken smells was comforting. I used to like to sit in the kitchen watching the rice boil, on the hob. The chicken would go in a clear plastic bowl in the microwave. It turned round inside, it was like watching television. I liked to sit and look at the oven door too, it was like a black mirror into another room where you could see through the glass dimly. It reminded me of the microwave., The smells and sounds of the kitchen are pleasant for a dog. The anticipation., the fragrant aroma of roasting, the sizzle of the fish in the fry pan, the soft thud of the over door opening and the waft of hot food laden air. The steady chop, chop, chop on the chopping board. If either Alex or Ivarna were at the kitchen bench, I'd be there, lying happily on the floor. Odd tasty bits would get flung in my bowl. Pan scrapings, bits of fat cut off the meat, smidgeons of cheese.

My meal have altered over the years. Now sometimes I get a fry up, sometime dog food. I used to get the "I haven't had time to walk to the shops too much work today," the piled high desk days, then she'd say "I'll get something out of the freezer for you Florence, scraps and scroungers day today" a slice of fried bread and bit of liver. I liked that best of all. Luscious liver, with a sausage on top. "You'll spoil her!" Alex pipes up as he passes. If it was steak night at the local pub, sometimes an extra little bag would come back for me in a pocket. A late night snack. I like my food, but I leave my meal in its bowl until they have finish theirs, to see if anything better or some tasty morsel might come my way, or be added.

"Is she like Ziggy? Alex asks on day. This is Ivarna's cue to show how well she thinks she knows me, "The basic chow character like Ziggy, yes, but she is different. Ziggy was a solemner more placid dog, she hardly barked, though she growled instead and she looked more intimidating so fewer people patted her. But she was less excitable

19

and tolerant when they did. They were much quieter round her and she was bolder. Florence has never learned to growl, and she has to contend with looking like a Teddy bear or a pet lion, so people just descend on her from all directions, often excitedly whooping and exclaiming, it must puzzle Florence. She has to be coaxed not to be alarmed by all the attention. But she's used to having her photo taken now, she almost poses, As soon as people see her the mobile phones come out."

The old adage says you don't judge a book by its cover. So don't judge a dog by its looks. When we lived in the town. I used to like to lie inside our iron railed gate and look out through the gaps into the street. Ivarna frequently had to come out to me when I barked, only to find people loitering, hands over the gate like leaning into a lions cage, trying to stroke my reluctant head. While I backed away head down hackles up barking at them. Unlike Ziggy I never learned to growl. I was never sure enough of myself to growl. Everyone understands a growl. They leave you alone if you stand calmly and growl, like Ziggy did. "If it was an Alsatian or a rotweiler or a pit bull, they wouldn't dream of leaning over the gate to pat its head!. They teach their children, don't touch a strange dog, because you can never tell how it will react, but they don't it teach to themselves." My teddy bear, lion looks make people forget the things they learned in childhood. I am like any dog alone at the gate, all I want is to be left alone. I guard my house in my feeble way. I cannot be won over. I'm not a family dog, not a child's dog. I have heard Ivarna say this many times.

Sometimes she glances out to check on me and finds me nose to gate tail wagging and silent, and someone standing there, that meant they had a dog with them. I was raised with dogs, and knew who I was in the pack. I have memorys of the great dark face, I know he was George, but he merges with Ziggy, just as Jenny merged with Ivarna, until I am not sure who was who or where it changed. There was Ginger, my twin, who I used to roll across the floor with locked-in-play combat and Grace my mother, and Muffin and little Fergus my brother, who was born smaller and not as healthy as the rest of us and was extra special for all that. How fickle the winds of fate. Had Fergus been a girl dog Ivarna might have asked for the smaller puppy instead. Or George, who at a distance was Ziggy's ghost again. Ivarna loved

20

me instantly, but it took me two months to really attach myself to her. I was cocooned by love, in my own dog world, but people and the clamour of streets were not part of my world. I learned to communicate with dogs well, in my little pack. I know which dogs I should be wary of and which to sniff nose with. But people make me uncertain. Now the past is all like a dream. Its as though I went to sleep and woke in a different world.

Some days when Ivarna came out into the garden to fetch me there would be a dog treat on the path. When you look like a teddy bear people want to give you things, they want you to wag tail and welcome them. I never do. Neither do I take food from strangers. You could call it a natural caution an instinctive reserve. When I was a pup every Friday a young man in a long light rain coat clutching his paper of fish and chips, would come off his bench and sit down on the ground in front of me, and try and tempt me with chips and crispy bits and curly tail ends. "One day Florence, I will offer you a chip and you'll take it." He'd have whole conversations with me, just occasionally he'd think on to say hello or bye to Ivarna too. I never took a chip. I had the feeling Ivarna might have done, if she'd been offered!. The woman at the pet shop who had kind blue eyes and a tired face tried me with a bonio, and various bits, but I wouldn't have any of either. In an outdoor café table in Newbiggin-by-the-Sea, a bonio and water bowl came out with the tea and cake. I did have a nibble that time. Many people train their dogs not to take tasty morsels from strangers. But in me this mistrust of people was inborn. I like a treat or a chip as much as the next dog, something inhibits me. Ziggy my predecessor was no genetic relation of mine but had the same instinct maybe it's a chow thing this mistrust of strangers.

Sometimes I find things, I found a bit of dead bird on the pavement, quick as a sniff it was in my mouth. I walked along proud as a lion, little black feathers sticking out of my mouth. Then Ivarna spotted it, I think it was the horrified look on the face of a passing girl that gave the game away. I felt my jaws being prized opened, momentarily it evoked the memory of being back at the vets, same sensation.. It was forcibly and disappointingly removed, I kept my eyes on the pavement in case there were any more bits of bird but my lead was shortened and I was yanked on. I kept it in memory for coming back, but she knew my intent. We went a different route back home that day. A dull route that took us past the school, where children like prisoners hung on the wire fence and gawped at me.

There is a subtle difference between a dead thing and a cooked thing, a made thing and a thing that was once alive, yet a sameness. One day I found a dropped sausage roll in the park. I sly-eyed Ivarna, both of us remembering the bits of bird, and I recognised the merest gesture of her head, she let me carry it in my mouth all the way home. I dropped it half way down our street. I picked it up, left little dots of slaver on the pavement. I dropped it again it inside the gate and didn't eat it, it lay there like the dog treats, but it was satisfying, like something I'd caught myself, the old instincts, dog instincts.

over the garden gate

Over the years we met a lot of people at my gate. There was Alec the golden Labrador, having his well earned day off work, he was guide dog and every Wednesday the owners elderly brother and wife would stroll past our gate with Alec on his own day out. He'd always give me a lick and wag. Its so nice to see a working dog have a day that is just totally for him, a day to run on the beach, to nose other dogs, to end up at the town centre, and like myself be petted and loved by all he encounters.. There was pixie who was the size and shape of a snow ball, eleven months and still not house trained. The paper boy whizzing past with his skate board and endlessly long basset hound that seemed to take an age to pass the gate. When Ivarna glanced out of the window and saw me at the gate, tail wagging, she knew it was another dog. If she heard my bark, she knew there was no dog, only a human, who had stopped to stare at me. I will never quit know why humans are so fascinated by my face.

The things we don't quite understand disturb us. Some people pass on Others linger. Lou always lingered. With light jacket and hedgehog hair. Face as creased as an old slipper. I always barked at him. Lou the alcoholic who loved animals but couldn't keep a dog himself, because of house rules and only ever spoke to us when he was drunk, but we got his life story in occasional episodes. He was not only alcoholic but a chronic depressive., He had the need to unburden himself and no one to talk to. Except the two men he lived in the same rooms with who had problems of their own, and one also tried to feed me treats at the gate, he didn't speak. Alcohol is only sometimes a problem, it is sometimes the answer to a problem. Once our silent friend who never normally spoke, came up to us on the traffic island as we were crossing the road, him from one direction, us from the other, and he spoke. " My cat died" He said simply. There was no else in the world for him to tell that to except a stranger and her dog. "That could be us Florence" She says later. " That will be us one day, all the people you meet, Florence, they are ghosts of yourself."

There are the hungry ghosts and unhappy ghosts and the ghosts of retribution and revenge, there are the ghosts of the past and ghost of the future and you meet them casually in your life in the form of other people. They are all shades of yourself, your fears and the things you have repressed. There was a core of uncertainty, that nervousness in me, that knows the instability and confusion in people too. Where ever we went, there was a certain bright happy kind of person, who would make a very determined bee-line toward us.

"I used to have a chow, I haven't seen one for years. Lovely dogs" The ghost of me in the future Florence, and me in the past before I had you, she'd say, future and past are one but they distort so we don't recognise it always. Once we met a woman who said she had an oil painting of a chow hanging in her house, the dog had belonged to someone in the family but he didn't know who It was, a kind of heirloom. A wag of a dogs tail, a kindly word, a memory evoked from someone's else's image can make a difference to a day. Ivarna wondered if she could paint me well enough to hang my portrait on the wall. But the work went on, the forecasts and the hundred different astrology readings she did, one after another, and there was little time to paint.

New chapters in life begin unexpectedly. A corner is turned and everything changed before you know it. We are at Wallsend to look at a house, Ivarna and Alex had an appointment to view. We were early and had walked from the house to the town centre, sat on the seat got some shopping and then back. I was slowing in my step. "You best go on ahead and meet the guy from the estate agents," Ivarna said, "I will walk Florence down slowly and catch up with you there". The house was along the banks of the Tyne. I could feel the cool river air, the strange atmosphere and sounds that such places have. Lots of industry and few houses. We felt very peaceful here. Like most dogs I am able to pick up on a persons moods, the unsaid things. Ivarna's mind was full of the past, familiar but older times that felt like a century ago before I was even born. I knew she has been here before, many times, it was ingrained, part of the cloth of her life.

Walking, in her mind was another dog. A dog like George my father, a big black chow. But where as my father George had a rusty iron tinge concealed in the black, this dog was pure shiny black.. I knew then she walked this exact same path with Ziggy. We paused at the exact same places, and it was like walking back through time. There was a surreal quality. A light fog had begun to drift up and we could hear the sounds of ships and the passing Metro train going to Hadrian road station, my lead was so slack, like Ziggy, for once I wasn't forging ahead, I had to be urged on. "Come on Florence, we have to hurry, not far now". I stopped at the corner about to automatically turn up the hill, though it was a corner I'd never turned before and there was nothing interesting there to draw me. Ivarna looked at me strangely. A quick yank and we walked on, not up the hill, a strange confusion was in me. Why would I want to walk up there, the question hovered in both our minds. The right path was straight on and its drifting smells of dogs and bushes was much more interesting. Then I knew. Walking Ziggy to the post box from the old house long before my time in Railway Terrace. With a pile of the clients' astrology readings to post, work was postal then, not email. Walking Ziggy along the grass by the metro line along to the Gut, as the muddy inlet from the river Tyne was called. Walking me, Florence, the same path so many years later, it was a ghost walk, Ziggy, who always limped a little after a short mile. I could see this dog in my mind. I knew its life story. Suddenly I was Jolted back to reality and snatched to a sudden holt. "Florence, your limping!" she was almost stunned. But it was my own eyes, not Ziggy that looked back up at Ivarna. We rubbed my leg and walked on. You can rest when we get to the house, she says, but we have to get there..

The house for sale was big and derelict. Alex's van was parked where we'd left it. But I couldn't jump up into it and Ivarna could not lift me in.. She thinks back, she could lift Ziggy but only just, and Ziggy weighed five stones, I am smaller and a stone lighter in weight but I may as well be twice as heavy for all the progress we make. We struggled for a few more minutes, my front paws and head were lifted on to the van, floor. So I was standing on my hind legs. Chows are very heavy but we have short legs. "Come on big effort, Florence" but she could not lift my back end up. Shoulder to dogs bum didn't work either. Neither did " lets hop in together Big jump." Side by side hand on collar, the way I learned to do stairs when I was little. Ivarna hopped in with my empty collar. I was still trying to heave myself up. We looked for a plank, there wasn't one. We looked for a passing man, there wasn't one either. "Oh well you'll have to come with me." she said. It turned into one of Ivarna's totally silly situations. Because the building was derelict maybe dangerous, a temporary solid board fence too high to see over the top had been erected round it, there was no way in. We scoured it. Nothing. No way in. Next to one of the boards was a bit of corrugated metal fastened over a wood fence.

"Oh I can see a way in Florence" she said. " Now you wait there, and don't talk to any strangers". She sat me on the pavement by the wheel and tied me to the van mirror . It was the only thing that stuck out. "Wait there Florence" I heard the clonk of her boots on the boards, the crank of corrugate metal being forced back, the swish and scrape of a long skirt being hitched up, the soft thud as she dropped down the other side, the slaps of dusting her clothes off. The mumbled, what a bloody nuisance, you'd have thought they'd have left the fence open for me!. Tromp, Tromp, Tromp. I am still craning my neck and head forward and turning it sideway to follow where she went in. The point of disappearance from sight. Then a bolt is pulled scraping like a shoe on stone, and a bit of the wood wall opens up. Out she comes, behind me! while I am still staring at the bit of The fence she went in at. In we both go. We find Alex and the estate agent outside in the overgrown garden at the back of the house. He looks down disapprovingly at me. "Was the van door not open?" He says. "Oh, I couldn't lift her up into it, she was far too worn out to jump." Ivarna is embarrassed at her own frailty. The thing is she is really quite strong, she is lean and hardy, and energetic and can thrive like a weed in even the grimmest of conditions but her back defeats her. Alex takes me back and heaves me into to the van,. I leave Ivarna behind to follow the agent round the rooms. Lugging me into the van takes a bigger effort than even Alex anticipated. In his mind I see the idea of him making me a ramp. Easier for all of us. They didn't buy the house.

that fearsome place

Next day I still limped with an intermittent lameness. I wanted to give my back leg a good chewing. An appointment was made the same afternoon at the vets. There are some places that bode you no well, the mind feels them like a hunger in the pit of the stomach, this was such a place. A dreaded place. I turned round to walk back out, but was turned full circle on my lead and in the momentary confusion I was back into the small room. "It's about a mile and a bit each way, not far for a dog but its twice what she normally walks." Alex explained as he lifted me onto the table I was far too heavy for Ivarna to ever lift now. I was after all a full grown chunky chow. My back legs were examined, knees, hips, feet. "You poor thing" she kept muttering. She had hair the colour of Ivarna's, but it was pulled tight back and smooth , she was strong and young and tall. "Do you have her insured?" Ivarna is of the opinion that best insurance is to tell the vet you're not insured, it avoids unnecessary operations and treatments. She shakes her head "No." she says.

"It might just be a sprain this time, it will wear off as she walks, but she is going to need both her hips and back legs operated on quite soon .We'll do this one first, the joints are slack, they will start coming out of the socket if we don't." "Florence has never had any bother with her back legs before," Ivarna said, "but she does trip, ever since we got her she's stumbled on her front right ankle, just occasionally." My paws and ankle were felt. "Nothing wrong with her right ankle." She said briskly, "she probably stumbled because of the back legs. But her front leg joints are bad too, so she will need them doing. "The vet said. " I'd get her insured if I were you. then bring her back and we'll book her in." The warning bells should have rang, the lighthouse should have flashed, but it didn't. Some people would have thought it was a kindness to give you time to get your dog insured if it needed expensive operations on all four legs. But Ivarna was numbed, horrified. They say the past comes back to haunt you. We went home, the ghost of Ziggy and the three of us, all rather depressed. "I don't want this dog to go through what Ziggy went through. I don't want her operated on," Ivarna said, "four operations are too many, when Ziggy died I promised myself if I had another dog I would rather have it put down rather than have it put through all that. To be operated on, and the operation go wrong, to have her die three months after it." The gloom was like a fog descending. As we left that fearsome place Alex touched Ivarna's elbow, "We'll get a second opinion, a different vet." After a week of intermittent hobbling my lameness cleared up of its own accord. All was well, for a time, we didn't return to the vet.

Three years went by happy years, my leg no longer bothered me at all, it was forgotten, receded into the warm haze of summers on the sand. Except Alex gave me a glucosamine dog chew each night and Ivarna had begun to give me a bowl of goats milk each night to "Strengthen your bones Florence." My walks were limited to under a mile. Except on the beach when we could walk for ages, and sit on the sand, and swim in the sea and never grew tired until we were back on the pavement, when we'd wend our way back down the long street home. We would walk in the soft sand often, "Build your muscles up Florence, that's why they train race horses on the beach." The vet was wrong then. No operations necessary. Or else the chews and goat milk had worked, strength in my bones and oil in my joints. My astrology chart was pulled out and duly written on. When one of our clients wrote about her own dog, his chart was drawn up too. Ivarna did cats and horses charts too, but mostly people. All grist to the mill. Happy days.

I remember winters of picking our way up the back lane the ice, so slowly, slipping and rebalancing, some dogs don't slip in ice, but I had to be careful. Ivarna had to be careful. Neither of us could afford to slip, Her back, my legs, we were a pair. "You should have seen us coming round the corner like two old codgers!" Ivarna said. I may have not have liked ice, but I loved the snow, the coldness, the freshness of it all. It was hard to get me back inside if there was snow the garden.

There were nice summer days too, Alex would sometimes saunter along with us if it was warm. We are outside the library one day, all three of us. Alex had decided to walk to the shops. I like these rare family walks. Its usually just me and Ivarna. I go straight to the bike stand and look up hopefully at Ivarna,. My lead hangs slack. "I wonder what she is doing that for?" Alex says, as I park myself beside the bike stand. "She is finding me a seat" Ivarna explains, "The bike stand must look like a seat to her." I'm good dog again. Thoughtfull little Florence. I am always finding seats.

We sit at a pavement café, I lie at the side of the table, I greet other dogs, nose to nose, they are walked on, after a quick word. The city dogs are mostly like me, showy dogs, civilized and friendly and have been brought up; to accept other dogs and people. It is a bit of a fashion parade too. We see the other breeds. The Dalmatians and the pugs and the husky's on parade. And little dogs with hand knitted coats. The people stop to stare at me, they ask about me. Its surprising how few chows there are. We learn the names of other breeds. Ivarna trots on without me, "just having a look at the market." Alex has another cup of tea. She comes back with a wide assortment of things stashed in a plastic bag, I nose it but I cannot smell anything interesting in it, it smells of cake, and coloured thread for the sewing machine, and paperback books, and leafy plants, and oranges. Off we go back home at a jaunty pace. Alex has my lead, he is firmer than Ivarna, so I have to walk on, not dawdle or stop and sniff. I have to go all the way home in one go without sitting down unshiftable, on the pavement. I keep glancing back behind me at Ivarna to make sure she's following on.. She waves at me and I wag.

A century ago, a dogs owner was referred to as its Master, or its Mistress, The astrological sixth house rules servants, employees and others who must obey. So this is why in older astrology books dogs were a sixth house matter. Dogs had a different role in the past. Some dogs are indeed still working dogs or kept to do a task, like guard the house, or keep the children company. The fifth house rules chance, children, leisure and pleasure, and a pet dog encompasses all of these things. Which is why more modern astrology book puts dogs under the fifth astrological house. A chow is not a sixth house dog, you will never make a servant out of a chow. You'll never master a chow.

I'm in the garden. Ivarna calls me. I don't come, I stand and look. I stare her down with toffee coloured eyes,. She calls again. I watch her gesture and hear her call. She goes in and leaves me, adjusts the pan on the hob, she comes out again, I'm still standing but have moved couple of curious paw paces forward. I get called again. I know what I'm meant to do, I saunter forward, in my own time, I stop to sniff a pot of hellebore, its smell hasn't changed from yesterday. New words are added to the call, like "hurry up", The teas cooking. She goes again to the cooker, back again, I amble forward, like a sulky teenager doing what its told but in its own time, and not wanting to look like its obeying. I pause again. I make sure she's watching first, then I turn and look back out at the gate. "No, this way," she calls, so I turn very purposefully in the opposite direction. I head right back to the garden gate. Looking round to make sure she is still watching. You have to show your owner who is boss from time to time.

I see her go for the little puppy lead, not the nice long walking lead. This lead is kept on top of a black lacquered Chinese cabinet near the big front door, If the puppy lead has to come out, it will be coiled round my neck before I know it. Its short and much shorter now that I am full grown, it keeps her hand close to my neck and its soft but it tightens quick and you cannot get rid of it by ducking your head and walking backwards. I don't dislike it, loved it when I was a puppy, and it took me for little walks from the front door to the back door, to get to know my street, but now its, well, it's the naughty dog lead!. Then its quick march you up the front step and in and if you stand still and refuse to budge there is a hand on your behind pushing you up and over the step. The puppy lead is mortifying it has a puppy stigma, it is an undignified thing for a clomping big dog like me. So I come in, "Its handy that little lead" Ivarna will say.

remember that first day?

I feel now as if I have been here all my life now. I hardly remember the long journey to Ivarna's house when I was given some rice and chicken in a little bate box for the journey to Tyneside. Ivarna had brought a tin of puppy food and bottle of water for me for the journey. I drank some water, but I would eat my own food, not the little can of puppy food. We stopped at many places, a soft little lead loops round my neck, and I was lifted awkwardly onto the grass, She found me difficult to pick up at first. Ivarna was use to cats and long legged puppies, I was short stumpy legged, heavy for my size and squirmed a lot, she was afraid of dropping me. Carried me bent double and wrapped herself around me like a coat . She lifted me from the back of the van to grass near where we parked. I bowled forwards like a cannon ball on a lead, quick and heavy, nose to the ground.

When I did not eat my packed food they offered me a bit of their sandwich, a drink of water, but my appetite had gone. Each time we set off I barked, to let my brothers, sisters and pack know where I was. It felt a distance away. I felt anxious, there was no answering bark. George my father, the pack leader should have barked, but he didn't. my mother, Grace had already rejected me. She was silent too. I couldn't hear the dogs, or Jenny, or anyone's voice, it disturbed me, I was alright with Ivarna I knew that, it didn't distress me being them in the van, but it was the silence, the lack of answering sound. At least there was no warning bark, no distress, or squeals, nothing to be alarmed about, but you'd think at least one dog would answer me. Each time we took off. Nothing. Just the "Shush, your alright puppy". The warmth of Ivarna's trousers and knees against my belly. I wasn't a Florence. I didn't have a name. I was puppy. I was orphaned.

I heard them talking about me, the unfamiliar accents. The length of the journey I could not judge. Humans can judge the length of a time because they know the journey finishes and they know what comes after, but a dog knows nothing, we could have journeyed forever because I didn't know what would come after. If I thought anything at all, I thought we would be back at Jenny's house at journeys end, because I knew no other world. But the traveling did end, late at night. I don't recall much about it. Only the tall, looming building we call home. The different salt smell of the air, the dank smell of the garden and path, and the moon flying in the sky. "I didn't think she would bark so much. I hope she going to settle in Ok. I might call her amber or honey. "I didn't respond to the names. With retrospect, you might think being an astrologer dog, I would have been named after one of the great astrologers of antiquity who Ivarna admires, like Ptolemy, Kepler, Sepharial, William Lilly, or Alan Leo. I know not who these people are, only that their names are uttered like hallowed words. But No, they are all boys. "Bitches are best, aren't they" Ivarna said, rubbing my neck. "you could put that on a T-shirt couldn't you!" "I don't think so," Alex answers, "well, not on your T-shirt, or mine." " I will just have to wait to see if she tells me her name" Alex said nothing, just raised an eyebrow. A few days onward Ivarna looked at me, I looked back into the human face "I think she's a Florence" Ivarna said. And I knew I was. I was a Florence.

In my puppy days I used to love to crunch through the rust coloured autumn leaves that were swept to the side of the path , they made a sound like the sea swishing on the beach beyond,. I'd seek out a pile and walk through them, Chomp, chomp, chomp, and Ivarna too, crunch, crunch, crunch. Then I'd go back a few steps and pee in them. The cracking sound brought back old memorys, memorys of paper. When I was a puppy the newspaper on the floor was for peeing on, except Ivarna had a bin bag under the newspaper, and a puppy liner on the top and she sprayed it with stuff that made you want to pee just exactly right there. Right on that spot. She always knew when I was going to use the liner. No matter how busy she was, meal being cooked, or Alex getting ready for his evening teaching job, or astrology to be done, she would yo-yo back and forth looking at me, looking at the liner, looking at the time on the clock. When I headed nose to the floor for the liner, she race me to it, my puppy lead would be lassoed round my neck. And it was quick trot into the garden, doors flung open, excitement of the outdoors, feet on cold path, instinctively headed for lawn, when I got up I was allowed to snuffle round the grass.

I soon knew to ask to go out, I would go and find her and dab her with my paw, often I asked, when I didn't want to pee, I just wanted a snuffle round the garden. I always knew the difference but Ivarna didn't, so I was taken out even if I'd just been and if " You cannot possibly want to go again," I was still taken out. "just in case." I heard her say. "I had her house trained in two weeks." Ivarna proclaimed proudly. I could have echoed that, its satisfying when your owner begins at last to respond to your every request, that when you know your getting them trained.

In my museum of memories there is a place some time after I was house trained. It was the time they bought me a dog bed, I wouldn't sleep in it, but I'd jump into it, and out of it, during play, and it was left in the far corner for me to get used to. One night I was playing with Alex, it was such an exhilarating game of catch the squeaky toy, and Alex was nearly winning, such excitement, I didn't want to interrupt the game, but I needed to go, the dog bed caught my eye, I went, jumped in and promptly peed right in the middle of my dog bed, to a chorus of "Florence! you naughty girl, I thought you were trained," and "Quick! fling the front door open for me, will you, and I'll run with her," and "No, don't pick her up, you'll get pee all over the place." "Too late, anyway, but put her nose to it and put her in the garden anyway." I was 'bad dog Florence' that time.

My puppy memorys are dimmed by the cloth of time. A week or two after my arrival. Ivarna said "I will send Jenny a card and tell her I have called you Florence, she will want to know that you have settled alright, and that your eating and happy. We'll walk down to the post box and post it, I used to walk Ziggy to the post box regularly when we lived in the other house, that was in Wallsend." So here we are back to walking Ziggy's ghost, and the empty house at Wallsend. The circles of life are ever intertwined in infinity, the paths keep crossing and we never quite see the end or the beginning of them, until we are there in the midst of it.

The days go on but some things are like a small river, they seem to fade out or their shadow changes, they go underground and reappear somewhere else, or come back in some other form. Sometimes they go underground like a covered well and you no longer know its there, until the whole of the above ground caves in. My lameness vanishes like the ghost, not to return for a long time, but a small brown leathery looking lump, like the pad of another dogs toe, appeared on my front upper leg. It was not much visible. " What's this I wonder?" For Ivarna it was a puzzle, but not yet a big concern. The lump did not go away. I paid it no attention. It got marginally bigger but at first not much. I gave it a lick occasionally when my nose came near to it, but otherwise I didn't bother. When I was due for my annual inoculations it was pointed out to the vet', The same vet', whose first question once again was, "Have you got her insured?"

The next week I had biopsy to find if it was cancer. The smell of ether and clang of doors and early morning being dropped off and not collected till late. That's all I remember. The waiting for the result. My joints weren't looked at or mentioned this time. It was as if the previous consultation had not taken place. But then it had been a long time before, and possibly forgotten.

I didn't have cancer. Ivarna was relieved, so pleased at the result, we all were. Then the vet said, "But we will have her in and remove it anyway." I could feel the puzzlement and caution thick in the air. "But why remove it, if its not cancerous?" The vet didn't answer. Ivarna persisted." if its not cancer, then is it just a cosmetic operation, isn't it. I don't mind what the dog looks like, if its just a blemish." The vet remained silent. Ivarna wasn't even sure she'd heard. She had turned away to her bench and busied herself doing what looked like nothing much. So Ivarna struggled to rephrase the question, she did not want to sound antagonistic or as if she was challenging the vet's wisdom, she was doing neither of these things, she just wanted an answer. She waited till the vet turned round to face us, "its so small. if you were going to remove it anyway regardless of whether it was cancer or not, then why *two* operations? why didn't you remove it there and then, and then send it to the lab? If you see what I mean," Still the vet said nothing. No explanation, no word was forthcoming. There is an old saying might as well talk to the wall, Ivarna looked at the wall but there was no answer there either. No inspiration. The only thing that drew an answer was "When should I make this appointment then?" Alex went to seek the van, while we paid the fee at the desk, and went outside. We didn't make the appointment, I was so relived to be out of the smell of disinfectant and death. Soon I was outside in the fresh chill air again, and hoisted up into the van. It growled like a great beast and spluttered into life and off we went. I hunkered down

34

for the short drive home. Conversation drifted comfortably like a warm blanket over my head.

"How much!" Alex gasped. "Well, I did think it was rather a lot." "It's a good job I drew some cash out of the bank in anticipation this morning." "But that's not the point, they could have took the growth out couldn't they at the same time. If they were going to take it out regardless of the result, its such a tiny thing? A general anesthetic cannot be good for a short faced little dog never mind two anesthetics." Ivarna says, but Alex has stalled, astounded at the cost. He has no idea what a vet can charge and is wondering about going back to complain, or "Get the money back." as he puts it. Already Ivarna is off talking to herself again, "I bought a chow because I like the chow temperament, the looks is a bonus. One of the nice things about animals, is they don't care how you look, or who you are. If you're rich or poor, if you're better than them or worse than them, they don't judge you or measure you, or cast you aside or accept you on all the superficial things that humans do, they just love you anyway." A short lapse into silence. I'd almost fallen asleep at her feet, but Ivarna had not cooled down from the vet's attitude towards her. "Do you remember, Alex, when Florence was a puppy, I said to that vet 'She drinks a lot', she didn't respond then either." Alex said, "Perhaps she just has a recorded message machine under the table '...is she insured?'...'make an appointment...', think she just wants our money, short of work likely."

Ivarna continues, "Maybe I should ask her how much she charges to answer a question? Or how much for common politeness? I answer all my clients' questions, all my emails, I can't ignore them when they were worried about something. It's sometimes frustrating being ignored, like being invisible, to never get answers, to spend half your life lost in the maze, groping about in the dark. I suppose it stands me in my clients shoes, when they come to me they are sometimes lost and looking for answers too, and I give them an answer, if I don't know, I say so. A chow gives you surprising visibility. Maybe subconsciously that's another reason why I chose this breed, to balance things. Maybe we choose all our dogs and cats for a subconscious reasons, they are small parts of ourselves, either repressed parts or reflections of the self. Florence is opposite to me in many ways and yet so similar."

Ivarna is reclusive, she likes the cloak of invisibility really, I know this in her every move, her conscious mind craves anonymity. She seldom speaks to anyone unless they speak to her. She likes being solitary. To walk in the street and not be bothered. There is nothing better than an empty beach, it's one of the places you haunt when you're alone, or a crowded the market where you wander anonymous among the stalls, your own table at a cafe. Listing to the music of the street buskers and bands. But with a dog you're never alone, we are such good company and you are visible in a nice way. You meet the good people, the nice people. Although fate can deal you a hand of negative people and bad situations at birth, and at times it outweighs the positive people and situations. It's the wolf pack that waits beneath you, with open jaws for you to slide into, jelous eyes, they are all on you, the people who joy at your downfall. The users and casual tormentors, the bullies, and the victimizers. Times when you have no friends. This is fate's measure, but in a dog like me you have an ally, the faithful friend, always there for you, you'll not find many of those in the human pack.

contrasts and reflections

Ivarna likes our rainy day walks when no one else is about, she grew to like the sunny ones too, where the park was full and we are accosted a dozen times, with "Can I take her picture?" and "Look, there's a lion on a lead." It forced her to be more outgoing than came natural, yet like me there is still that hesitation. Life is contrasts, she knows millions of people more closely than anyone ever could, the other invisible people, I feel them round us, the clients. We know all things, the room is like a confessional, we know their lives, their thoughts on everything, their problems, we know more than they do, because we know their astrology chart, the lighted path into their future. Some of the clients have been corresponding with Ivarna since before I was born. Once it was letters, now its emails. There are always new clients but we keep our old ones too. Remarkably she remembers them all, just as she knows all the flowers in her field and the clients are scattered as wide, all over the world, yet here in our home place we walk and I am the only star, and she walks at ease, unknown. Life is contrasts and reflections.

I haven't written much of our long summers, chows are thick warm coated and like husky's we prefer the cold. I am double coated and when I molt Ivarna sits and combs my grey white undercoat out. She calls it my little wooly vest. The summer is hot and walks are slow and steady but shorter. I stop and stand still to breath, my mouth gets moist with dribble. We sit more, though Ivarna's back is somewhat better these days. I sense it in her livelier movements, the little things. She is less like an animated match stick, more willowy and stretchy like wire. I'm lethargic in summer, I lie around in the yard more. We have a big high walled north facing yard. it is cool and partly shadowed by the tallness of the house. Its duller and though sheltered by the high wall, it is colder than the front, but Ivarna wants to make it into a walled garden. Already it has tangles of Russian vine hanging down from the top of the wall, and purple aconitum, a spindly ash tree, a tall bush and a white climbing rose. There is a little grass plot for me to pee on, but I often go behind the wheely bin if they are not watching. Alex parks cars and a boat and the van, in it. He props up old doors, bits of wood, ladders, other debris and odds and ends around the edge that are interesting to sniff at, full of the story of where they have been before.

Ivarna does not like them at all, you'd think they had a malevolence. She likes a tidy yard. But I like to sniff round, amongst the lost tennis balls, and fallen leaves and broken clothes pegs, and dropped socks off the washing line. The rotted smell of peeling wood doors with traces of coal dust and curling leaves is pleasant to my nostrils. Ivarna is fussy about smells. In the evening, head up, I sniff the fragrant air, the curry smell drifting over from the restaurants on Ocean road. Now there's a small Ivarna likes.

Alex has plans in his mind to build a workshop or garage down by one of the roller shutters. They are sketched out on drawing paper. Ivarna doesn't like the plans either, "It will take up all the yard Florence" she says, "what about our garden", but she likes the plans better than the old doors. Plans she says to me will never happen, they get blown away like autumn leaves, but doors are too heavy to move. Only the bit of yard at the bottom of the steps by the back door has been transformed. But there are a few flower tubs added now and its creeping along. When the yard is empty of cars we run round it with a tennis ball on a string, well Ivarna does, I do a perfunctory trot, after her, and she runs and ducks and twirls and flings the ball off at a tangent, so it bounces off a wall in an unpredictable direction, and once or twice I run and catch it, just to please her. I run the length of the yard and she applauds and pretends to grab my tail as I pass her, it's a good game. Then we get the sweeping brush out and I jump on it and catch it in my mouth and give it a good bite and a shake as she tries to brush the yard. I learn its called the sweeping bush, or weeping brush. Then we go in.

In the summer afternoons, She stands at the top of the yard steps. two Coffee cups, one in each hand "We're going into the garden, Florence," I know what that means, I heave myself up, lumbering too quickly and clumsily up the steps, to the words of "careful Florence." I trot inside and we go down the passage to the other end of the house and out of the front door, a cup is passed to Alex, if he's there if he's not its "Wait there Florence," and she goes running upstairs quick as like a lighted match stick, to remind him his coffees out. Sometimes its repeated a few moments later. Then we are all sitting there in the sun, with the purple buddleia tree in full bloom in front of us. Our terraced house garden is small, and sunken, it has a Cherry tree, a Salix, a

38

Laburnum, and a high hedge comprised of a variety of flowering bushes, and Poppy's as big as dinner plates along the side of the red brick path.

There are rugs on the floor for me to walk on, there is a gap between them, and my feet slip on the laminate a bit. I am used to this but I forget to slow down. "Careful Florence." I hear this a lot and I know what it means and it reminds me, makes me hesitate. But one night I fell, I fell hard and I didn't get up. Ivarna rushed to me, sat on the floor beside me, stroked my head. I didn't struggle up. I didn't attempt to move. If I had been a teddy bear I would have knocked the stuffing out of me in that fall. I hardly knew how it had happened. We just sat there for a while, until I was ready to go, Ivarna helped me up, I think I was Ok.

We liked the new vet a lot more, he was old, experienced he wore an apricot coloured turban and a white tunic and baggy trousers and had a lined face and an ease and kindness etched in it. The face of wisdom and experience. He never mentioned insurances, and his waiting room was more bare, minimalistic and basic, it was light blue painted wood panels, and hadn't changed probably in twenty or thirty years. It was in the front room of a converted terrace house, and felt clean and spacious with a high ceiling. He was quick and apt on his computer, had the most modern drugs. He instilled complete confidence.

"How did she fall" the new vet asked. "Well I was letting her out her for a pee, I was in front of her, I heard her skid on the mat, she fell on the laminate". " No, I mean did she fall like this?" His hand made duck feet motions. "Did her legs splay out at angles?" "No, there was heavy thump, and when I turned round she'd she pitched forwards on her chin. Her front legs were straight out in front, her chin was on her paws, her back ones under her." He nods. "If her legs spread eagle out, it means the joints are slack and the ball will come out of the socket. But if she pitched forwards, its opposite. The joints are stiff, they wont come out of the socket but she could break her leg. You and me, we get old, we get arthritis, we fall, we cannot up so easily. It is the same for a dog." He stands back looks at me from a distance. "We can try these pills. Bring her back in a week to see how she's doing. I give my own Labrador these pills. They are very good, but some dogs have side effects, so we need to make sure she tolerates them". The growth on my leg is looked at with interest. Operations talked about. "There is risk in the anesthetic," he says, especially for a dog like Florence, if its not troubling her, It is best left alone." No one was smiling as we left.

Miracles do happen, the tablets that he gave me, Alex called them Rimadyl (carprofen), had me back on my feet by the next day. To think one moment I couldn't get off the floor, the next I was running round, or as much as a chow every runs round, we are not boisterous bouncy dogs, we are the laziest of breeds really, but I felt back to normal. I had everything I needed, a good home, a trustworthy vet, park, beach and a big yard and a garden whose gate I could look through. I was an enviable dog.

Ivarna thought back to the first vet, the woman who would have had me in for four separate major leg operations by now, and be a bit a bit richer by it, and now an additional one for my growth. She felt happy for me, but sad for all the poor dogs put through unnecessary operations, It's nice to know vets are not all like that.

dogs are better than people

If I seem to drift through time and place in this story, it is because we have lived in different houses and had different experiences. To an astrologer time is important but to a dog time is no time and anytime, it is all one and the same. I wake from sleeping, I know I have been chasing something that eludes me in the wet grass but I wake and it has gone and the bushes and dank green fronds of in front of me have gone. I have run through them and out the other side, there is, only my claws clicking on the floor now as my eyes open, only the warmth of the room around me. I have run through the door between worlds, one world intersects with another and you slip through them. Waking and sleeping. Like night slipping into day. How I get from the hunt into the room I don't know, how I get from past to future, and back to present where I don't know, it is the way the worlds weave in and out, through movable boundaries Time is an illusion.

"Aye, dogs are better than people." a unknown man we have never met before in tartan trousers and fur hat muses sadly, sighs half to himself, he has left a pub, and a bunch of drinking friends straggling far behind and pauses at the sight of me in passing. His face shows that its as much a wistful disillusioned introspective comment about the company he has walked away from at the pub door as about dogs. He stoops down to pat me on the way past. Ivarna nods and smiles in agreement at his remark. There is no more to be said. Sometimes a fragment can tell the whole story.

That one remark is stored in Ivarna's mind because it is all our life stories, it has an essential truth about it. A dog never tell lies. It doesn't tell you all the lies that people tell you about yourself. The lies you believe all your life. Lies like your not good enough, not clever enough. Not attractive. Not worth bothering with. The lies that those who are worse than you are better than you. That the liars and cheats and backstabbers and cruel mean minded people are better. That you have nothing to offer. Nothing to give the world. Not worth speaking to. Not worth anything, a dog will never tell you those lies. A dog knows your worth, it welcomes you. It values you. People tell you these lies from your birth until your death they tell you it, in their different ways and actions. A dog tells you the truth, it tells you that

41

you can be loved for who you are. It never judges you. It wont desert you, or turn on you when you've lost everything in life, when you have nothing more to give. It wont make use of you and leave you behind when there is no more uses to be made. When there is nothing to buy kind words and company or the illusion that you are not alone in life. A dog is at your side whether you're right or wrong, it stands by you. When there is nothing left in you, and the humans leave like rats from the sinking ship, the sturdy Chow will still be standing by.

The man's remark, so simple but to the point comes in useful one day. She is on the great Metro. I was at home that day so I can only unravel it from the clogging cloud of thoughts that silt up her human mind. It was close to Christmas, and a dark haired woman strikes up a conversation. She is depressed, not quite tearful. There is a bleakness in her that has walked beyond things, but hasn't quite emerged out of the other side of the empty road she is traveling. She casts a few remarks round to other people in the carriage, they answer. Other passengers ignore her but their ears are all stretched listening and finally she settles in the seat across the aisle from Ivarna. She is like an oil painting that Ivarna cannot quite remember, all shadows and light, fine features, dark curled hair, if it were longer she'd be like a pre-Raphaelite picture, head drooping, dark dog-like eyes. She tells Ivarna she hates Christmas time. Ivarna is not happy so there is an instant un spoken affinity. neither woman is happy. The woman tells of her kids who never visit but live near, how Christmas is such an empty holiday. How she feels like ending it all, the closer it comes. It gets worse each years.

Ivarna's tells her that the only thing she really likes is walking through the park on Christmas day, feeding the swans at the lake when there is not a soul around. Then walking on the deserted beach. They talk for a while, Ivarna struggles to find the right words to help, but Ivarna is so depressed herself that year she muses that if she makes friends with this woman they will probably end the day with a suicide pact on the sand. But she is an astrologer she has no friends, she knows that people don't come to her by chance, they are sent to her for a reason, that everything is fate. Then the tartan trouser man's phrase comes back to her, like a homing pigeon to roost. "Animals are better than people" Ivarna repeats. The old man across the isle who's been listening half turns, looks about to join in but doesn't get the chance. "Yes they are." the woman says. Then inspiration comes, "I've got a lovely dog," Ivarna says. The woman smiles, flickeringly like a lighter running out of fuel, she remembers her own dog, her own horse, there is a shift, the air is lighter. She tells us about her horse, her dog. "You can trust a dog, you cant trust people." the woman says. "A dog can give you nasty bite," the man says, "it can kill you if its big enough, I wouldn't trust a dog." Ivarna smoothes out his remarks, "Only mad dogs bite, but all people kill you, don't kill you physically, but they kill you emotionally, by inches, till there is nothing left in you to kill, they all do it in the end," the woman nods, the man is washed out of his depth, the woman knows exactly what is meant, "but you haven't got to let them grind you down," Ivarna continues, placing a gentle hand on the woman's knee. "No," agrees the woman, "haven't got to let them win. I'd like another dog". "You want to get yourself down to the cat and dog shelter," a thin boy in a black hoody chimes in. A world of unlived joy and sorrow before him, but his eyes are helpful, hopeful, "I got my dog there, it would have been put down if I hadn't."

At Jarrow the woman gets off the train just a mite more cheered. We never saw her again. The next few days when Ivarna walked me down to the town Christmas tree and back we looked at the headlines in the local paper, newsstands. No suicides, we thought of her a lot, we will never know the end of the story. But Ivarna knew intuitively that once she said "I've got a lovely dog" and the woman recalled her own long ago, much loved spaniel she had got it right. It felt right. It was up to the woman and chance now, the small myriad chances you meet on any road can be the decider of your fate. Even a kind word or a harsh one, or a new idea or an old memory can be a turning point. Later it seemed karmic. If the woman rescued a dog it would in turn rescue her. By saving its life she'd be saving her own.

Animals, dogs and cats and other small creatures have much to give. All animals deserve to someone to love them. Just as all people do. They don't always find it. All dogs have a destiny, all dogs have a life story. What kind of dog is destined for you? I have chewed this page out of one of the corners of Ivarna's astrological note books; If the ruling planet of your fifth house is in the ninth house, a breed that has its older ancestry in a foreign land. If in the fourth house, a breed originating close to home. If in the sixth or tenth house, a working breed. The eighth house, a rare extinct or reintroduced breed. A dog whose zodiac sign is the same as your fifth or sixth house, a breed who falls into the category of your planet mars house or sign is a good start too.

the seventh gate

Some years were uneventful. The growth on my leg did not bother me much for three years, it hardly grew at all. But then it seemed to accelerate, it had grown from the size of an acorn to the size of my nose, for a long time it resembled exactly that, a second little leathery brown nose. A snitch on my elbow. The first few times the new vet seen the growth, his words was echoing Ivarna's thoughts; that if it wasn't bothering the dog, better to leave it alone, because an anesthetic was a risk in itself, and that's how it had been. It wasn't painful, it did not get in my way, but in fits and starts it was growing bigger and worse showing no sign of stopping. Twice now, once when I fell on the laminate and then once a year later when I had begun to limp unaccountably and hobble. I had been given the miracle pills. Once again and within a day I'd gone from a hobble, not just back to a normal walk, but I'd bounced with new health and new energy, I jumped up on things, that I'd never been able, or even inclined, to try to jump onto before. To her utter astonishment and total delight I'd actually twice jumped up onto the park bench and sat next to Ivarna. The second time Alex was with us and gave me and Ivarna a stern look of disapproval. He doesn't believe dogs should sit on seats. "Well, the park is almost empty, it is not as if someone else is going to sit there." She sat with her arm round my shoulders.

But then the little nose on my elbow grew very quickly, a little leather purse. It was my seventh year now and Ivarna had hoped the growth would be so slow as to live out my lifespan without it increasing much more. That wasn't to be. It began to get convolutions, to resemble a world war two hand grenade, or small, tight, round Easter egg. Then of a sudden it seemed like it happened all in a day, it hung downward, revealing the dark band of skin that tied it to my leg. Ivarna and Alex thought it might come off like a sole from a shoe, it seemed now to look easy, to be hanging, only attached by a smooth piece of skin as if the whole of the growth was outside and non of it inside my leg. But it didn't fall off. We were back at the Vets to see if he could shrink it, or cut through the skin and remove it.

This time he had an orange turban and a dark almost black dress suit, tie and waistcoat. Ivarna liked his Indian tunic and baggy trousers better, but its rare to see anyone so properly dressed these days and he looked every bit the old family Doctor.

"What about removing or maybe reducing the growth, it didn't grow before but suddenly its increasing a lot." My growth was examined, it was, as Ivarna had found herself, to be only attached to my leg by a piece of skin. But it wasn't the good news Ivarna had hoped for. "On another dog, or a different breed of dog, it wouldn't be a problem", he said, "but for Florence, it is a different matter, any operation at all is a serious danger for the dog. Florence is an old dog." That was a statement not a question, Ivarna shook her head. "She's seven." "Seven?" the vet said, almost doubting the accuracy of Ivarna's response. "And how long have you had her?" "Since a puppy, of about ten weeks old." The vet was puzzled. "Seven." he said again, as in disbelief. He went over me twice again, all my joints. Spine and shoulders were felt, legs flexed, the stethoscope came out. Nothing was left unexamined. "Seven years you say?" He kept standing back from the table and looking at me, rubbing his chin. It was as if he expected some clue he had missed would become obvious to him. "Some dogs can live as long as fifteen years. But Florence is not going to live that long. You have to start thinking of Florence as an old dog. You have to start treating her like an old dog. No running about. She has to take her time. She is already twice her chronological age. She has arthritis in her spine neck and all four legs. There is no safe operation for Florence. The growth is big but its not the problem, there would be some blood loss. It's the breathing, the anesthetic, that is the concern". The stethoscope was put away. "It is more than fifty percent certainty she would die from the anesthetic if she has the operation now. But then again if she has to come in as emergency when she is older still its eighty to ninety per cent certain she won't survive. So its up to you." Ivarna looked sternly at the vet, shocked, and declined his suggestions of a risky operation. The odds were too high. "Come on Florence, I'll take you home." She thanked the Vet, and told him she'd keep me as long as I was happy and just hope the growth slowed down.

If I was twice my age, that meant I was probably in my last months of life. I was already on borrowed time, for which chows never lived much more than ten. If the growth didn't grow too fast, I might get my natural life span, "Even if she only gets another year or two, it's a

46

reasonable age for a dog. Dogs don't know the time, they don't know if they have a long life or a short one, they live in the moment. So long as they are happy that's what counts." Ivarna said she thought I was happy. She didn't realize I was listening, sensing what was going through her mind. I felt sorrow descend around me in that small room, like a thick blanket that blotted out all hope. The shadow of the future lay heavily on us. I was seven, seven is supposed to be a sacred number, a mystical number, but I can tell you for me it was a terrible number. I had never known Ivarna be so depressed over me. There is depression and there are worlds without hope. This was one of them.

"Tell you what, drop me off and I will walk her home, she hasn't had a walk today yet and I need some space in my head." It was almost dusk. We walked along the grass and tree edged cycle path, near the church, but so slowly, me stopping and standing still every few yards. Ivarna slowed from despair, both of us looking for a vacant seat to rest ourselves. There was only one, just inside the churchyard gates. It was beginning to get dark so we didn't want to go too far. It was a well trodden path.

Ivarna hardly noticed the boy get off his bike. Children are sometimes intuitive, sometimes sweet, sometimes awful, but always direct. "Has that dog got cancer?" the little boys voice piped up. Small whey faced, grey coated. His bicycle left aside by a bush. "No, but she's quite ill." "Will she die." "I think so, yes." "Its on her leg isn't it, can they not operate?"
"They could, but she's too old to have an operation." They said it was fifty-fifty she would survive". The boy strokes my chin and chest with small deft hands, he looks like a boy from another era of time, face soft with shock, he already knows my name. He knows you can die of cancers, but he didn't know till now, you can die because your too old to be operated on. "I used to have a dog," he says, and already we know his story, and why he was drawn to me, why he notices dogs legs when other people don't. The street lamps come on, and we get up. The boy goes for his bike. "Will you get another dog?" Ivarna asks him? He nods very solemnly. "I don't think I'll get a chow, though, or a retriever."

We moved house that year. We moved last winter when it was cool and we walked in the woods, and I settled in quickly. I don't always settle in strange houses. I gained energy. It was full circle, I was born in the countryside, now I'm back in the countryside. Instead of the gulls we have crows, the black sheep scavengers of the sky. When we have a chicken for tea Ivarna puts the carcass bones out for the Carrion crows. It's a different way of life. The grass was like a soft green carpet cushioning my feet, it makes walking easier. The sky high pylons that overlook the garden sizzle in the damp, for the first time we see the stars again, at night its pitch black round the back of the house, so we never go up there. In our other house you could not see the stars but it was high up and you could see all the city lights spread out like a sequenced lace shawl. I like the darkness of course, the wolf within me, whose eyes shine like a cat's in the dark. But they don't let me out the back in the dark because they cannot find me. It's a torch job, I still don't bother to come when they call, because I cannot see the point, they don't want anything when I get there, just told to lie down and wait for tea. So after dark, if I need to 'go', I'm in the little front street garden, where there is still a friendly street lamp lighting the way all along an empty road. We had a fox in the town, we used to see him, we have a fox in the country too but we never see him, we just hear his weird sudden cry at night and finds bits of dead things and feathers.

I feel fitter, but the growth has got bigger it is as big as a bunch of grapes. Ivarna didn't expect me to live much more than the dreaded seventh year. But I am approaching my tenth birthday now, the date is on my yellow card Jenny gave to Ivarna, "We don't know your time," Says Ivarna tapping away on the computer, "so this is what we have to do." Ivarna continues talking while tapping, as much to herself as to me. "If you don't know the time or date of your dogs birth, then the best you can do is treat the nativity as a business chart and erect the chart for the time and date when you bought him, or her in this case. The astrology that applies to a human chart doesn't work on a dog's chart, its all slightly different but not many astrologers have researched this in a serious way. They simply adapt human definitions and human zodiac signs to dogs."

Ivarna has researched more deeply. This is what she does in her spare time, she researches things. I see her at her desk late at night, the lamp behind her, book of planetary tables, called The Ephemeris open, looking at the stars and days events. Making notes on computer, cup of coffee to hand, or with note paper, and pen in hand, books piled to toppling height on the floor, around her desk. The desk is a flat white table with an array of disheveled papers and clients charts spilling over onto the floor. She sits in the shape of a Question mark, intently, hooked over her desk. Her hair is mixed shades of yellows and golds, from golden brown to straw, and darker brown bits. Its like a candle flame an unruly mess flaring all over the place. She wears no make up. Old clothes, once decorative no longer fit to be seen out in, are worn to work in, oddly thrown together and in winter, if the room is cold, an outdoor scarf is added and multi-coloured long socks "Good job my clients can't see me, Florence" she says plodding across to me in her slippers.

just another day

Last night there was a thunderstorm. The night sky was menacing to me, like a dark threat of doom, and even now that I am old and slightly deaf, the thunder rolling and rumbling round unsettles me, I cannot sleep, I pitter-pat round the house, the click of claws on laminate and wood, keeps me company in my silence. What do I fear? I ask myself. I don't know, it's something old instinctive, something not right with the world. How can Ivarna sleep through thunder and raging wind storms. I go to the great sleigh bed where her pillow is, and I shove my muzzle in her face. I'm rewarded with my name. "Hmmm...Florence...." I go away, not much reassured.

The lightening flashes don't unsettle me. I grew up in the city after all, a street light outside the window, car lights illuminating a dark room, then gone like a lighting flash in slow motion. I am a creature that walks by night but I don't fear the light, or the moon, or the twilight, or the street lamps, or the darkness at all. It's the sky, the vast dome of the ambient. It's the thunder, the wind, most especially the wind. The Earth, the bigger house in which we all live has the charged smell of the storm, the piquant struck matchstick smell of electricity, burning in the air. I hear the rattle of the wind descend from every direction. The sinister growling of the thunder, circling round the house, now near, now far, like a menacing dangerous predator hunting us down. Me and my little family sheltering safely in this house. But I'm not sure we are safe. Something could creep out from any corner of any room and strike with the speed of a lethal snake. Humans think solid walls are secure, that's why my owner sleeps oblivious to the storms she thinks she knows more than me, her only concern is if the chimney has loosened or if any slates have come off the roof. But dogs know other things, timeless primeval things that go back before houses and shelters. The night seems baleful and endless but by morning the storm has almost cleared.

I'm let out. I like to play outside and run in the wind. Though I cannot run so far these days, it's like a little sack of beef mince is strapped to my leg. But I like to feel the wind tickle my tail and blow through my hair. When I canter or have a caper round the garden it brings joy to everyone's face that echoes the joy in mine. I only hate wind storms at night when there are no distraction and when I am inside the house. In the lofty terraced house we used have you didn't hear the wind much, but you'd feel it come down the chimney. When we moved to a solitary house, the wind sounded weird and different like howling animals. Ivarna liked the sounds, I took courage from her calmness. In her childhood she lived in a corner-end terrace house. She used to lie in bed, listening to the way the wind played round the corner, and in the telephone cables strung high across the street. Drifting off to sleep it sounded like the far away howl of wolves, I heard Ivarna describe it like people singing hymns in the distance out at sea, a heavenly choir, or of some old Russian folk music being played in the Siberian wilderness. The music of the night, it was comforting to her.

Outside I take my customary stroll round the garden, I peep through the glass door of the kitchen to see Ivarna standing at the bench. The coffee aroma that so delights humans and mystifies the rest of us drifting through the crack and then the whiff of biscuit, the clink of cups and slap of feet, then she's gone. Face to the door, I bark and bring her back. "Come in Florence, if your going to bark" I go in. I don't bark. She carries cup to desk and the day's work begins. The first astrology case of the day begins at breakfast. There is no break until a certain amount of work has been done. I settled myself under her desk grunting as I get down. Nose still up to check if the chocolate wafer is still with the cup. A quick glance into my dark amber eyes, the shuffle of paper, the burr and bleep of the computer and work begins.

I lie silently, then roll back onto her feet, "Keep still, Florence, I have to get on with this Karma." I listen to her grumbling at the computer's inefficiency at keeping up with her typing, the words coming out mixed up, muttering to herself at client's letter,
I can almost hear her thinking. I might not say much but I have learnt a lot dozing under her desk here. The first reading of the day is a past life reading. In an astrology chart the ascendant is calculated from the minute if birth, it symbolises the doorway into life and the twelfth house which is the house behind, or before that door, is the house of mystery and unconscious memory. Things about our previous incarnation show up here. Ivarna had previously told the client that from the planet and aspects in her twelfth house, she thought she had a brief previous life that ended as a child who'd been murdered at about

the age nine or ten by the man next door, and the body put under the floorboards of a passage. Ivarna had told her a lot of things about another past life. But it was this small detail of the short life that had caused the woman to immediately e-mail back. Ivarna's reading had astounded her. She told Ivarna that from the age of ten she'd begun to have recurrent terrible nightmares. She'd wake in a unfamiliar bedroom, an extremely tall man would be standing at the bottom of the bed. She would wake terrified, in a cold sweat, with no clue to what this was all about. The nightmare had continued to the present day. "The man might not have been so tall," the letter read, "but if I was a child at the time he would have seemed much taller, that explains so much, and the terror of him." The dream had no ending, she always awoke at that point. This is characteristic of past life dreams. They are recurrent and the dream doesn't have an end, it's cut short, it just stops there. The age in the present life at which this recurrent dream begins is often significant to the event in the past life. "Will the nightmare stop repeating now that I've found the explanation, or is there something I have to do, something unfinished, should I pray for the murderer's soul, because I've moved on into a new life but he hasn't?"

Ivarna tried to work out the past life date from the chart. The client thinks it the eighteen hundreds, because there is a gaslight on the wall in her dream. But Ivarna cannot get an exact date. She thinks it's later, early 1900s. The astrology reading indicated that he body was under the floor boards. So she suggests to the client she learns about house building, not all houses have floor boards, not all have room under them for a child's body. The client felt the past life was in Lancashire. Because she once visited a place there and while it was not familiar it had an effect, like a memory she couldn't quite recall. She tells Ivarna about her own research. Ivarna is fascinated. She hopes the client will come up with something solid that confirms the truth of the chart. The therapeutic effect of the reading was hopefully that the nightmare would stop. Karma is not just about past lives, it is about themes and recurrent situations that we face again and again within out present life until we find the underlying cause. If your relationships always end in the same kind of situation, or you budget carefully but always fall into debt, it may be a karmic theme. Anything recurrent that you cannot find your way out of is a karmic theme. Saying a thing is karma, is not the answer. It's a label, its like saying its meant, you then have ask yourself, why is meant, what I can I do to resolve it. Its often some weakness of character. Occasionally its paying a karmic debt by doing a good deed. Karma readings do have magical effect, like the nightmare stopping. But deep karma also requires diligent work on your own character, self awareness, or understanding of others, before the karma is solved life can be happier. Karma readings are only one of the many astrology readings that keeps Ivarna busy.

Part way through the morning I smell warm milk and cereal and hear the lovely hum of the microwave. The microwave has been music to my ears since puppy days when I used to sit in the kitchen of the other house and watch my chicken going round, coming out in a big round plastic bowl. A slice of bread would be sopped in the warm fat and jelly and dropped like a wet dish rag into my bowl. Then at proper meal time, some chicken meat and rice. Fond memorys. I get up. The faint aroma of hot tea. Alex is having his breakfast. I potter back through to the kitchen. I wait. "You'll have to wait, Florence." I know. I wait. I am rewarded with a walk up past the back of our house and into my field, I amble round happily, I do a big smelly one in the long grass at the edge, I follow the trails where a rabbit has run. I sniff where the pheasant and foxes have been. I sneak a drink out of the dirty water puddle Ivarna likes to call The Pond." Florence you've got fresh water in the house, get out of that, its not good for you." I ignore him. What would Ivarna or Alex say if I nosed the coffee cup or tea out of their hands and said, 'Get out of that, you've got fresh water in the tap'.

There is no immediate damage after the storm. Ivarna's Sambucca tree and apple tree are still standing, the fences are still up. It's autumn and the field looks yellow and windblown, the weeds and grass bare, like it's had a bad haircut. I have lived here two years. After the first lightening storm we woke in the morning to find a small pine tree was split in half. Before we moved in a pine in the same spot had split asunder and part of it had fallen across the garden and remained there through the most of the summer. Lightening does strike twice then. Ivarna said. When I find myself out in a storm, I hasten straight back, if I'm being walked in the woods on the lead and a storms impending I hasten ahead, I go the full length of my long lead stopping to turn round every few seconds looking back anxiously at Ivarna, who doesn't hurry at all. When we get back to the pavement and cycle path that leads to our house, my lead is shortened in, so much that I pull Ivarna along like a husky pulling a sledge, but I make a sudden stop, I wait to get my breath back. My head gets patted and she waits 'till I'm ready to go again. In winter and autumn we walk a long way, in summers the walks are shorter, summers are lazier, you lie round more when you're a chow. The crows make for the bird table, some bread has gone out. Alex has gone in, and I wander back down to the house and content myself to sit by the house, thinking a dogs thoughts.

Ivarna works on, and three soul-mate readings get done. Everyone wants a prediction of who their soul mate is, what he will look like. If he will be kind or ambitious, or stubborn. If he is dark or fair. If his cheeks are hollow, or he has a scar on the face, it is the detail they love. For some people the prediction is pure entertainment, a bit of fun. How can you predict someone's soul mate, or even their next boyfriend? Its done in traditional way. Even if you know nothing of astrology, the revival of old traditions delight the senses. But Ivarna is dedicated. To know that you're not alone in the world, that one day you will meet someone who understands, is a great thing, because, so many people are alone. This is what makes astrology worth while. This book is about the astrologer's dog, my life with Ivarna, but Ivarna is astrology, and so its unavoidable that I have astrology in it, to talk of Ivarna is to talk of astrology, and I see it all in pictures, all the planets have pictures. Saturn is the skeleton, the reaper. If you have transit Saturn aspecting the area that shows your future dog, the one who will appear in your life under the transit will be thin, lean cadaverous. Even if he's a chunky breed he will be thinner than usual. Less so if Saturn is in a meaty sign, like Taurus, then your future dog he will be big boned angular and strong as a bull. The more you work on the chart the more detail can be had. I watch Ivarna work meticulously. My mind is cloudy and I don't know the details of things she does, I know its like looking back and forward in time without any boundaries in-between. An Astrologer dog learns patience. I must sit and wait until the work is done, then it is my time again.

There are more than zodiac sign that give pictures, the degree and the fixed stars that have a meaning too. The star Algorab, the crow, for example, it is considered unfortunate, brings illness, said to cause

55

poverty lying and scavenging. If a dog has this fixed star badly placed strategically in its chart there is danger of it not only straying, but being a persistent strayer. The life of a vagrant's dog, or an outcast dog, going from one home to another, never settled. And lean bits in-between, full when the star become aspected. In human chart it can remain on a semi material level and can be more positive, such as having a Romany spirit guide, or you may be intuitive and know which way the wind is blowing. Ivarna was acquainted with a good Tarot reader once, who had envisaged her 'Spirit Guide' as a raven. She was like a black crow herself, small and hesitant, with a hoarse voice and hair so black and sleek it was like polished marble, and always caped, like wide dark coats, long red painted finger nails, and wellys! The star was connected to her ascendant, she was a born psychic, and an excellent tarot reader. She knew no astrology, had never had her chart drawn up, but without ever being aware of it, it was if the crow symbol had subtly become part of her life. Like an inner totem animal. She was eternally youthful, like the wandering soul, yet sometimes tired and needy, like the beggar, but needing sustenance of a difference sort from what the world has to offer. It's a better star for a human than a dog.

The day is fine and dry, and Ivarna takes an hour or two break. Out we go. I follow her up to the allotment. I'm not allowed to help water the plants, but I make my little mark by the polytunnel door. The raised beds get weeded and inspected. Two or three big creamy potatoes are dug out of the ground for the dinner, and a cup of small sweet tomatoes from the tunnel. Old bean stems are pulled up and put in the compost box, which I had watched Alex make out of a few pallets, when its full up, he is going to make another one next to it, he says. Then we are down to my field and Ivarna digs, and turns over some of the clods of ground. Tells me its good exercise. Tells me she is going to knock a garden out of this field. "Hop in Florence," she always says when the big orange wheel barrow comes out, and I laugh and wag my tail and walk merrily along, skipping a bit. I drop off to sleep watching her weeding and planting. Then I amble up and look through the glass door of the workshop to see what Alex is up to and its, "Hello Florence," hello Alex.

Ivarna's back at work. More readings get done." Cannot keep the clients waiting longer than is necessary." This is our regular day, our routine. But there are more interesting days when I get taken in the van and walked on the beach and go beyond the extent of my longest lead so that Ivarna follows me into the sea, water slapping over her feet, there is nothing like cold sea water down your boots and the flapping wet hem of your skirt on your legs, the salt wind on your face and the music of the sea. I have to keep her on the lead of course, or goodness knows where she would end up, we wouldn't want the lass to go too far out would we. But then Alex takes the lead and we stand clear of the water, watching Ivarna disappear into the distance, miles along the shore and back. She picks up a pebble that's like a natural work of art, turns it over in her hand, stands and looks out to the horizon, the ships the sky, the far distant light house. It's a different beach we go to now with a different meaning. I get sand in my toes and sea water up to my hackles, my wet hair stands out like and animated flue brush and quick as a sneeze I shake myself over Alex. What fun we all have. Even when she's not on the lead we haven't lost Ivarna yet, she catches us up as we wander back. As we walk a husky runs up, then a spaniel, and its wag tails, sniff noses and on we go. A young curly coated dark dog has his ball in his mouth, drops it in front of me. We guess that he's a lab-doodle puppy. I'm reminded I'm too old to play with him, but Ivarna throws the ball for him and off he runs, all legs and ears and his owner stops and talks about dogs and weather, she catches sight of my disgusting growth, but does not mention it and we all walk on.

She has to be firm and say "That's far enough, Florence, remember your legs, you have to walk," and other things like, "you're soaking wet Florence, your hair's all over the place." When I look at her I could echo all that. Wherever I go she follows, that's what a lead is for, you can follow your dog, or it can follow you, sometimes it doesn't really matter which. Some people walk their dog, Ivarna doesn't walk me, we go for a walk together, we always have. Other days they go out without me and I sniff her skirt or trouser hem and her shoes to see if she's been to the beach without me.

The day has turned out mild, still and sunny now, so Ivarna and Alex eat their evening meal on the outside table in the garden, while I lie in the grass. "Eat up Florence, there s good girl." I don't eat up. My meal is in my bowl but I wait to see if there's any tasty scraps from the table that will be added to it before I eat. Sometimes I get a walk up the street before Ivarna has her meal, but it depends on how I'm walking, these days, my legs aren't always so good on pavements and on the hot summed days I labour and lumber a lot and would rather just lie outside the kitchen door. But there are still plenty of cool autumn and winter days when I can plod along.

Alex has a cup of tea. Ivarna doesn't, an astrologer's day is a long day, there are always people waiting. She goes back to work. She will work another hour or two, then we finish for the night. Its exhaustion all round. I get my little bowl of warm goats milk. They have a pot of milky coffee, the TV goes on. I dose off on my big blanket near Ivarna's chair. I wake up, and go and ask for my dog treat. The packet rustles temptingly, the stick pokes out, its waved in front of my nose teasingly, I grunt with anticipation, and as it edges towards me I pull it from the packet, and off back with it to my blanket. Its a big dog glucosamine stick, good for my joints I'm told, I know it's tasty. Sometimes I get a Denty Stick instead and sometimes a bone.

Alex returns to his computer to send the day's work out, and prepare the charts and emails for the next day. I have a final potter round the front garden before my bed time, the night brings out the moths and the dampness from the earth, the smells that are not there in the day, night scented flowers, damp juniper leaves, wet earth, the blackbird sings in the dark, a small bird or something scuttles in the hedge, then nothing, nothing moves, the traffic is silent. Its different from our city house, which was all sound, and street light and human voices, people shouting, drunks singing, youngsters running and swearing, cars starting, doors slamming, the town hall clock donging, the faithful hours for the insomniac to count in the middle of the night. Here the street is very still, and on a clear night you can see the stars that Ivarna writes about, the constellations. In the early night its like a Vincent van Gough picture, and later still the sky is inky dark and the stars look much higher in the heavens and the milky moon looks down. At somewhere between half one and two Ivarna goes to bed, and I'm left to settle back on my blanket, "Goodnight Florence," and then we start all over again. Just a typical day in the life of an astrologer's dog.

back to work

Life goes in circles, it revolves round Ivarna's work. Her clients, her researches. Her life also revolves around me, or my life revolves around her. Ivarna is always cleaning, but the house suddenly is never clean, there is a cloying smell like cantharides, a sweetish stench, fetid, pungent, unclean that lurked in corners. It seemed be emanating from me, I licked myself clean. I had to lick and lick again. My tea pot handle tail is drooping down instead of standing up and I don't feel well. My big soft chequered blanket is put in the washing machine and hung over the line outside in the sun to dry. Ivarna is down on the floor wiping my awful, smelly sagging growth inch by inch. All the doors and windows gape at us. Alex's relatives have decided to come and see the house. "If they notice the smell I'll just have to apologize and explain that my dog is not well, after all they must have all had smelly dogs in their time. Well they must, mustn't they?"

The relatives have met many times me before, but I am still an object of curiosity. Its not a good time to smell. Its a not a good time to bark. I do both and Ivarna over compensates. "Dogs are such good company," Ivarna tells the in-laws, "cats are nice too, I had cats for years and years but you can go for a walk with a dog." We are all standing outside in the drive like a raggle of tourists waiting for the guided tour. Ivarna pats me, she is about to add what a sweet nature I have, but is interrupted, "Its not a very friendly dog is it?" They are all looking down at me. I stare boldly right back up at them. I give the sort of stare that small children get being told off. I manage a gruff half bark that sounds like a cough, and is reserved for such uncertain occasions.

"Not used to visitors, that's what it is, but she's friendly enough, sure of herself too," Ivarna says, "I can walk past anything with her, any other dog at all, and know she's never going to be any bother. That's what you want in a dog isn't it?" She waves her hand at me, open fingered like a pigeons tail. Usually I wave my tail, when I see that particular hand motion. She does secretly think I could be just a tad more welcoming to people in a situations like this, but I'm a chow, a big, chunky, surly chow, and a smelly chow. I cannon ball past them, bowling my way through them and pushing ahead of them into the house, I resist all efforts to leave me and my smell behind in the garden. I am a dog that knows its own mind. Ivarna doesn't try to coax me back outside, she knows I won't go. So she sly-eyes me and discretely opens a window. Alex manages to shut me out after we've all had the tour of the garden. "Ahh, look, you've left Florence out." One of the in-laws opens it for me, I dart in. The relatives don't hang around for long, wonder why?

Over the next few days, I get worse. I begin to look ill. My tail is down, my head is down, my appetite puts me off my food. "The growth on her leg, its really smelling bad. I think she's scratched it, there is a clear liquid oozing out." It was bathed in various things, with herbal names that smelled like garden plants, and pine trees, and my leg was wrapped in a sock. The growth is much bigger since we saw the last vet at the old house. "We'll take her to the local vet." Alex insisted, Ivarna tried to hide her concern.

The new vet is Scottish, dark, young, Celtic looking. In green Scrubs. I wait patiently while I am examined. I am used to being prodded by now.
"I'll give you some antibiotics, and we'll book her into our vet hospital to have that growth off... no, its quite a simple operation, it looks big but its only held on by a skin." Alex tells her what the last Vet said, the state of the dog, the anesthetic and that now I'm three years older. They have been happy healthy years Ivarna did not think I would this long, she thought I would die of natural effects or have me put down to end my agony. But the growth is very big now and infected, Ivarna thinks this could be my last visit to a vet. "No, it shouldn't be a problem," the vet is saying, "she has got a bit of arthritis but its not that bad at all, her leg joints are ok, her heart's ok." The appointment is made for me, in a vet hospital near Morpeth.

Ivarna and Alex take me away, mystified. Ivarna speaks first," How can she be pronounced virtually in her last year of life two years ago, 'twice her chronological age' he said, and now she's Ok, an operation no problem? Who do you trust, who do you believe, he was a good vet he gave her good tablets. He seemed genuine. And that first vet, the woman who would have her four leg joints operated on ages ago, all, unnecessary according to this vet. The one who did the biopsy when

60

she could have removed the growth at the same time, and they both said the opposite didn't they. She said her leg joints the ball and sockets were too loose., would slip out. The man said the opposite, he joints were too stiff. This vet says there not much wrong with her joints. A small bit of arthritis, but good for her age. Who do you believe?" Ivarna chews the question over all week.

That man was a good vet, but he really believed she was too old for a operation, what if he's right, what if he knows something this vet doesn't? Ivarna is not cheered. The light never dawns. Hope can be false hope. Once again she's fumbling in dark waters looking for answers. She doesn't look at my chart. She doesn't look at her own chart. All roads leads to the same destiny, she thinks, we just come by different routes. I will die of the anesthetic, or of the operation, or worse, a few days later of its after effects. I hear them talking, don't really understand but I know what they are saying, that my chances of survival are weak, but if I don't have it I might die a lingering death, or be put down most likely. I should not be listening in, I don't want to hear. All roads lead to the same destiny, we simply choose our way and hope it's the easiest one.

I was sad, not just for myself but for Ivarna, and Alex, what must be going through their minds. The last kindness you can do for a pet is not to let it suffer, to have it put down and believe me it is a kindness. The thing about an old dog, or old person for that matter is that it is never, ever as clear cut as that. So this is for all the judgementalists who think they know when someone else's animal should die. For all the people who think they know wants right and wrong in other peoples lives. Neither life nor death is as neat and tidy, or a simple decision. Time was catching up with me. Death had turned a sudden corner towards me. None of it was neat, non of it tidy. There are good days and bad days, and there are days of hope and days of no hope, and it fluctuates. Do you have the dog put down today? Or tomorrow? Do you do it now, when he seems a little better, or do you wait till he has got worse. Can you trust the vet's opinion, or can you not? Is the dog happy, is it not? How long do you wait, how long is too long. Even when you disregard your feelings and put the dog first, it is not a clear cut decision. There is no one to tell you if you are right or wrong. Its a dark tide where you cannot see daylight. Its asking people and not getting answers, its knowing that you don't know enough, and that you are guessing. The steps you take are stumbles.

To some problems there is no good solutions, that is the only truth. This is one reason astrology is so popular, it gives answers, but even astrologers don't have all the answers. Ivarna did not look at the charts. Did not look at my chart. She did not look at her own either. There are times when you just don't want to know the future. Fate had taken the decision out of Ivarna's hands. I would live or die in the operation, as fate or nature intended. Already I could feel her withdrawing from me. She at least did not have to choose, fate would decide now.

She handed my lead over to the vet, watched me walk away through the door. The terrifying, light green, thick door, that's slaps shut like all hospital doors. I know Ivarna is convinced I won't survive, she will work in the allotment, there is nothing wants doing up there, but she does it anyway, trying not to think about me. I am taken away, soon fast asleep, dreaming, I can see Ivarna walking away pushing her wheelbarrow, Alex on the beach in the distance, the gentle waves just trickling in around his boots. Can't see me there.

dreams in the rain

I dream of being out in the rain, I like the rain, it seeps to my skin in cold tickles. When I was a puppy I used to play with the spout in the back lane, I'd pat the water with my paw as it cascaded and splashed and jump back and forth, like the water was a living thing. I was trying to catch it, like a rat in a hole, the water in the drainpipe spout was alive, and elusive. Nose and front paws down, tail in air I fought with the water, such an entertaining interlude for a wet afternoon. I never could quite get my paw up the pipe. Ivarna would stand smiling down at me, hood half obscuring her face, shoulders huddled, one hand cold and white knuckled clamped round the lead, the other plunged into her pocket for warmth. I loved to amuse myself this way, it was such a merry little game. Then on the best of rainy days going round the back corner of the old terrace where we lived the gutter would be full to overflowing, and I'd plodge along toes tingling against the current. Feet like soggy slippers. I'd peer down the grid of the drain, to the chuckling and swirling sound of the water. I'd want to go back along, but " Enough is enough Florence, we're both drenched."

So home we'd go. Through the gate, the tree dripping down its wetness on us. I didn't mind. The big front door had usualy shut itself. So Ivarna would knock and we'd wait for Alex, getting more drenched by the moment. The collar would be slipped off, and Ivarna's shoes and jacket discarded like waste paper, and while this was going on the words, "She is wringing wet, come here, Florence," Alex would say, "let's dry you off." A huge, red fluffy towel, my special very own towel would be draped over me and, ooh! the lovely sensation of being rubbed dry. I could put up with that all day, its better than when I get my daily brush.. I'm an old dog now, the spouts and gutters no longer fascinate me, but I still love being dried off with my big towel, when I've been out in the rain. Its worth getting wet for.

The Allotment has a high fence, and big wooden gate. It is a sheltered private world in there. Ivarna doesn't want to be in the house to get a phone call that will say I won't be coming home, that I didn't make it through the operation. The phone always instills its own dread anyway, like a knock on the door in the night. Alex went to the vet's, alone.

63

Ivarna is still in the allotment when Alex's van pulls through the big iron gate at the side of the house, she watches the van drive in, waits while Alex closes the gate, then walks down to meet him. Although she hopes he has a smile for her, she's expecting bad news, the worst of news, and has composed herself. It's a bright, sunny afternoon but her steps are slow, solemn, as if the lighted match of her being has been blown out. While her yellow hair fly's up in the breeze, there is no sun in her heart. As she approaches the van Alex appears from the side, is he smiling?

"I'm back home." I shout, but it comes out quietly more like a creaking door, not a whine or bark or a husky howl, but the wordless sound I make when I want something. A tails wags, my mouth hangs opens. She's sees me, quickens to a jaunty pace to greet me with a pat on the head, a big but uncertain smile. I have a fluorescent orange bandage on my leg, it is inspected gingerly then a careful cuddle. Alex gets a hug. "There you are, Florence, you're back." she says, giving out a brief sigh.

I'm still a little groggy, but I want to go straight for a walk. I am walked on lead up to the big wooden gate of the allotment and back, its far enough, the effort weakens me. I want to canter round my field like a cart horse, I look across the field with hungry eyes, eyes still big and glassy from the drugs.

I get to the back door of the house, I'm helped over the stumbling step. I feel the brush of my hair, the tickle of my ears as my collar and lead come past over my head. They sit comfortingly on the kitchen floor where I can see them. Some dogs detest a collar and lead, but I love mine, it's a reminder of all that's good in the world.

I'm exhausted, doped, the world is both strange and familiar to me. There is chicken and rice in my bowl. Just a tiny amount, I pretend to be off my food, no appetite, not hungry, look at it, look away, look at Ivarna, eat a mouthful, a morsel, not keen, look at the cooker. "I've treat for you," Ivarna says, then, to Alex, "when she smells it cooking her appetite might come back." A plastic bag comes out of the fridge, the frying pan is plonked on the hob, there is a familiar 'plop' in the pan. I smell the heat of the hob in the air. I lick my chops in anticipation and lie watching the cooker, "fried bread and liver, Florence, your favourite!"

It is much later when my chart is dug out, medical notes made on my stars. Transits are looked up. I can sense a book on real astrology for dogs in the making, not just zodiac signs astrology, I hear Alex on the stair, popping his head round the door he says, "I think Florence could write that book, she has watched you long enough, probably do a better job than you." Ivarna stops scribbling for a moment, but says nothing, just scribbles on.

I feel I should end with a dramatic statement, like 'the following week Ivarna lost it and jumped off the Tyne bridge' but she didn't. More like 'and lived happy ever after'. Life went on, as usual, as it does for an astrologer, and her dog. My operation and recovery were a complete success. I feel better than ever, to the amazement of Ivarna, and Alex. The move to the country has been a revelation, we all have found a new lease of life, I walk on the beach at Seaton Sluice often, always wanting to stay there forever, until I am home and the crackling of the stove and smell of the meat in the oven reminds me of where I belong. And if we had never moved here we would not have found that vet, who of course I hate, I hate all vets, but I suppose I have to thank them, they have been amazing.

let's do astrology

Ivarna is back to work, a chance to go through her books and update them. She has a shelf of notebooks in her room, they are really just old hard back diaries, but meticulously hand written, over many years they record nothing of Ivarna's life, but all her research on stars, planets, aspects and events. There is one on astrology and health, accidents, ailments. There are case histories and careers, love, death, marriages, transits, eclipses, tarot and other arcane subjects. As I have a few moments to spare I will take this opportunity to let you into a few secrets of astrology, I have picked up quite a lot while lazing under Ivarna's desk, but don't tell Ivarna, she will have me doing her job if I'm not careful.

Most dog astrology books refer to human Zodiac signs and apply the same traits to the dog, and it doesn't work. Because dogs are not human, of course, a dogs character is in its breed. The oldest part of the dog is its ancestry; astrological eighth house sign and aspects, and though the dog has been a pet for generations down it will instinctively retain what's its ancestors were bred for. The choice of breed is more important with regard to character and behaviour than the choice of zodiac sign. The eighth house of your dog's chart along with its breed will show what it has inherited. Remember the Zodiac signs are just a fragment of a dogs chart, they are not the whole picture, and various aspects or planets in your dog's actual chart may alter or cancel these generalities out. Let me explain;

The Aries Dog

Aries dogs will have possible teething troubles, bumps and burns to the nose in puppy days. Voracious appetite, can be hungry again soon after eating. Can be easily trained by treats. Skin irritability, eczema, mange, skin allergy, kidney infection, heat exhaustion. Dull eyes in old age, hip joints and tendons trouble in old age.
If your sign is Aries, this Aries dog will be slow to learn and difficult for you to command.
If you are Taurus, the dog may be more aggressive or nervous than you'd like. One way and another it will cost you money.
If you are Gemini, a good adaptable companion

67

Cancer, apt to stray.

Leo, a shared karma, a lively companion.

Virgo or Libra a good companion dog.

Scorpio, it may have more health problems in its life time than you hope for, but a great companion and favourite.

Sagittarius, a happy playmate for you.

Capricorn, a good house dog, and house guard a good practical choice

Aquarius, a reasonable match any trouble will be from neighbours, rather than the doing itself.

Pisces, you will always be spending money on the Aries dog.

The Taurus Dog

Obesity, disobedience. Kennel cough, fits in puppy hood, heart, kidney or spine weakness in old age.

If you are Aries, this dog will eat more than you expect, will be costly, and need more care than you envisage.

Taurus, the dog may be more stubborn, unwilling to obey you, and harder to train than previous dogs.

Gemini, an insecure dog, less confident and adaptable but may be a good guard.

Cancer, an excellent stable companion and friend, a sociable dog a good family pet.

Leo, a dog the demand attentions, needs to be worked or trained.

Virgo, the Taurus dog may stray.

Libra, an affectionate dog, loving but may stray or not live long.

I your sign is Scorpio, the Taurus dog will be a dull but steady companion.

If Sagittarius, the dog may have health problems.

Capricorn, a good house dog, companion a good practical choice

Aquarius, a good choice.

Pisces, will fit in with your environment and neighbourhood.

The Gemini Dog

Gemini; lungs and nerves, tubes, ducts. Movements quick and nimble. Joints. Quick to lean but doesn't always retain it. Fretful anxious, picky with food, allergies.

If you are Aries, this dog will have two distinctly different barks or sounds. A clever dog, and will like children.

If Taurus, the dog will have a changeable appetite, likes treats and can be trained with them.

Gemini, the Gemini dog is not for you. You will likely change it for another breed altogether.

If Cancer is your sign then a Gemini dog will be timid or moody, you will have difficulty in understanding it.

Leo, a sociable dog and good companion, whom your friends will like.

Virgo, a dog that likes training and working, attention, and doing tricks for you, may stray

Libra, may stray or need longer walks than you anticipate.

Scorpio, may not live long, or may involve more vets bills than you expect.

Sagittarius, may have power struggles.

Capricorn, possible healthy problems.

If you are Aquarius then a Gemini dog will be a good choice.

Pisces, a good house dog. Won't stray, won't need as much exercise as you think.

The Cancer Dog

Cancer: house training, urination in puppy days, Mouth, teeth and eye. May be inclined to eat bad things. Kidneys, diabetes, stomach digestion.

If your sign is Aries, the Cancerian dog will be a good house pet or family dog.

If Taurus then your dog will get on with your neighbours.

Gemini, a good greedy eater, not fussy with its food.

If you have Cancer as your sign this is not the ideal dog for you.

Leo, a timid dog, may be reluctant to go out much.

Virgo an easily house trained dog and a good companion

Libra, a good dog but will like to be trained or worked

Scorpio, the dog may stray or be unsettled when you are not home.

Sagittarius, may be a weak dog. Inherited traits from mother.

Capricorn, a practical choice, easy to master but not ideal.

Aquarius, a good choice. May get you noticed too.

Pisces, a good rapport and understanding with this dog.

The Leo Dog

Leo; spine. Lively in the early afternoon. Skin inflammation, strong odours. Liver infection.

If you are Aries, a excellent outgoing companion.

Taurus, this dog will have a few healthy problems in later life but a good dog for you.

Gemini, a reasonable companion but demands commitment.

Cancer, a lively disposition that may be at odds with what you really want.

Leo, a head strong showy dog but not really the one for you, has the looks but not the temperament

Virgo An easily trained dog.

Libra, a good dog, outgoing will impress you are friends.

Scorpio, may be more aggressive and demanding than you expect.

Sagittarius, will need a lot of exercise, playful.

Capricorn, a good choice for a working dog.

Aquarius, an opposite dog top your own temperament but may work advantageously

Pisces , a reasonable choice. But may have more energy than you. will keep you fit and improve your health.

The Virgo Dog

Virgo, immunity, house training and bowls, digestion, allergies. Anxieties. Worms and parasites. Chet and lung. Hips in old age.

If you are Aries, the Virgo dog will be good obedient companion.

Taurus, this dog will be a good friend and practical choice.

Gemini, a reasonable house dog, easily house trained.

Cancer, not much mess, clean habits.

Leo, a fussy eater, possible food intolerances. Vets bills with this animal.

Virgo, you will expect too much from the dog, so it won't come up to your hopes.

Libra, a rather timid dog.

Scorpio, will behave round friends or family, but a Virgo is not your ideal dog.

Sagittarius, you will find the Virgo dog easily trained.

Capricorn, a good walking dog for you.

Aquarius, possibly inherited health weakness.

Pisces, less perceptive than you hoped for.

70

The Libra Dog

Occasional vomiting, or feeding or whelping problems in puppy months. Travel sickness in puppy day. Needs to eat little and often frequent thirst Drinks large quantities. In adult years, eyes, red eye.. Youthful in nature, retains something of he puppy but the appearance ages quickly. The mouth sags and the eyes become wise and expressive. Learns by copying. Digestion poor the appetite comes and goes. Flatulence and constipation, in old age hips, joints and tendons. Deafness in age. Libra dogs in general are affectionate, protective, with a little streak of stubborn independence.

If you have Aries as your zodiac sign this partnership will work well, an affectionate animal who will look to you to master it.

If you are Taurus, a good companion

Gemini, a playful companion but may be one or two unexpected turns of event

Cancer, the dog will settle well and fit in with your home life

If you are Leo then the Libra dog is a good choice.

Virgo, it will cost you more money in its life time than you anticipate.

Libra, a good companion dog, this is one time when own zodiac sign can work well.

If your own sign is Scorpio, it may be a more retiring, less confident dog than you hope.

Sagittarius, a good friend indeed is found in this dog.

Capricorn, a good practical choice.

Aquarius, may be inclined to stray and may need more exercise than you hoped.

Pisces may not live as long as you want.

The Scorpio Dog

Scorpio, anal glands, excretion. House training problems, eating bad things, Reproduction. Heart, ankle ligaments. infections. disobedience inherited traits.

For Aries people the Scorpio dog will have hidden inherited traits.

For Taurus, a reasonable pet but you wont always understand its actions.

Gemini, A good pet for you and good working or trainable dog.

Cancer, An excellent pet and companion.

Leo A rather quiet house dog.

Virgo, the dog could stray, go missing or be stolen.

71

Libra, there will be hidden expenses and costs you are unprepared for.
Scorpio, the dogs temperament will clash with your own, not ideal.
Sagittarius, may go missing, may be timid or too easily intimidated by you.
Capricorn, you will have difficult understanding this dog.
Aquarius, a trainable dog, will have a hidden purpose in your life.
Pisces, may stray or end up a long distance from you.

The Sagittarius Dog

Sagittarius; lungs and nerves. Hips. Worms, loss of appetite, fussy with food eats strange indigestible things. Feet, claws.
The Aries owner could find this dog straying, might need longer walks than you think.
For Taurus, it will have hidden inherited traits.
Gemini, a reasonable pet but you won't always understand its actions.
Cancer, a good pet for you and good working or trainable dog.
Leo, an excellent pet and companion.
Virgo, a rather quiet house dog.
Libra, the dog could stray, go missing or be stolen.
Scorpio, there will be hidden expenses and unexpected costs.
Sagittarius, the dogs temperament will clash with your own not ideal.
Capricorn, may go missing, may be timid or too easily intimidated by you.
Aquarius, you will have difficult understanding this dog.
Pisces A trainable dog, will have a hidden purpose in your life.

The Capricorn Dog

Capricorn; joints, legs. Exema skin chewing. Hair pulling. Diabetes or kidney in old age, dimming of eyes. inherited traits.
If you are Aries the Capricorn dog will be easy trained, a practical working dog.
Taurus, the dog will need a good amount of exercise but won't be beyond you.
Gemini, it will have hidden inherited traits
Cancer, a reasonable pet and affectionate house dog, A good choice.
Leo, a good choice for you temperamentally, but a little dull.
Virgo, an excellent pet and companion.
Libra, a rather quiet house dog, a good choice.
Scorpio, the dog will be a little tying, and dull on walks.

72

Sagittarius, there will be extra expenses.

Capricorn, too much like you to be suited.

Aquarius, may be a good guard.

Pisces, a trainable dog.

The Aquarius Dog

Aquarius; spine, waking up at night. Barking, throats problems, reproduction.

As an Aries owner your Aquarius dog will be a friendly sociable pet. Not the right one if you are looking for a guard.

Taurus, the dog will be easy trained, a practical working dog.

Gemini, it will need lots of exercise but within your capabilities.

Cancer, if it's a pedigree, there may be something amiss, or non-pedigree in its ancestry.

Leo, a good choice for you temperamentally.

Virgo, an excellent pet and companion.

Libra, a reasonable pet and affectionate house dog.

Scorpio, an impressive or quirky house dog.

Sagittarius, this one will get you noticed on the lead.

Capricorn, a shy dog but colourfull, a show off in private.

Aquarius, not a good choice, misunderstandings will hinder training.

Pisces, a timid but trainable dog.

The Pisces Dog

Pisces; Neurosis nervous disorders, trembling. Immunity, Nails and claws.

If your sign is Aries you will over domineer or master the Pisces dog. You are suited to it, but its not happy with you.

If Taurus, the Pisces dog will be a friendly dog, may like the water.

Gemini, easy to train will be a people pleaser.

Cancer, May more require more exercise you'd like

Leo, could be weak or have inborn health faults.

Virgo, a good companion.

Libra, a sociable pet and a good choice.

Scorpio, a companionable dog,

Sagittarius, a quiet house dog.

Capricorns will find this dog likes walks.

Aquarius, may be fussy with food, apt to be spoiled.

Pisces, not suited temperamentally.

73

Compatible Zodiac Signs.

If the dog's sign precedes your own zodiac sign, the dog will be more withdrawn, less confident or possibly more nervous fearfull or aggressive with strangers than you would like, may have to be coaxed more not such a good socializer. May mimic or mirror your own subconscious issues. May help you overcome those issues as you work together on them. While a dog whose sign comes after your own will end up costing you lot of money one way or another, hopefully will be worth it.

A dog of the same zodiac sign will not generally be a good choice. For dogs are different from people. It will bring out your worst traits and be difficult to control. Though it you may work on issues to do with self control, and facing your own more negative traits, a dog of the opposite sign however will generally work better than you think.

In general the following signs are compatible. But it really depends on your individual chart. If the dog's Neptune conjuncts your mercury or falls in your twelfth, the dog will pick up on your thoughts but it only works if you can interpret its thoughts.

Thank you for taking the time to read this book, I hope you have enjoyed it as much as I have enjoyed writing it, and I know Ivarna has found the experience enriching, satisfying and sometimes a bit of an ordeal. All dogs have a destiny, and it was mine to write this book. This astrologers dog is no ordinary dog.

You might find out more about us at the website or Facebook, just search for Ivarna the astrologer, and her dog, Florence.

www.ingramcontent.com/pod-product-compliance
Lightning Source LLC
Chambersburg PA
CBHW071928020426
42331CB00010B/2766